I would like to dedicate this book to my mother, who despite all the hardships we faced managed to give me the greatest gift of all: the freedom to chase my dreams, and to Paulina Castro, the love of my life, who from day one supported me in my relentless pursuit of those dreams.

First Montag Press E-Book and Paperback Original Edition November 2015

Copyright © 2015 by Jonathan R. Rose

As the writer and creator of this story, Jonathan R. Rose asserts the right to be identified as the author of this book.

Montag Press
ISBN: 978-1-940233-25-3
Jacket and book design © 2015 Niall Gray
Cover and interior illustrations © 2015 David Rogers

Montag Press Team:
Editors – Nick Morine & Charlie Franco
Managing Director – Charlie Franco

A Montag Press Book
www.montagpress.com
Montag Press
1066 47th Ave. Unit #9
Oakland CA 94601 USA

Montag Press, the burning book with the hatchet cover, the skewed word mark and the portrayal of the long-suffering fireman mascot are trademarks of Montag Press.

Printed & Digitally Originated in the United States of America
10 9 8 7 6 5 4 3 2 1

CARRION

Jonathan R. Rose

MONTAG

Here is a claustrophobic landscape of heaped flesh, ravenous vermin, and human monsters. Each body in *Carrion* is possessed by a maddening hunger that Jonathan R. Rose describes viscerally and graphically. What begins as a brutal, relentless effort to fill the stomach becomes another kind of ravenousness, one emotionally rooted but still debilitating. This novel is starvation captured on the page.

Alana I. Capria, author of *Wrapped in Red* and

Hooks and Slaughterhouse

I chose this book because of its unrelenting bleakness and visceral action. Unique and soul-shattering -- one of a kind.

Nicholas Morine, author of *Punish the Wicked* and

Cavern.

This stark, minimalist novel is about existential flesh munching and bone-crunching that conflates heroism and monstrosity. Sure, 'it is a dog-eat-dog world and the first bite counts.' All about the free market, El Chapo style.

Peter Wiesner, author of

Xtremus: a Bionican Quest in the Wake of Cybrergeddon.

CARRION

Jonathan R. Rose

1.

From pure darkness came blinding light as the jaundiced eyes of a monster opened and gazed up at the large, luminous sun. The golden glow stared back at him warmly. After taking a deep breath of fresh, floral air, he was besieged by an insatiable hunger.

The intensity of the hunger astounded the monster, for it clutched, consumed, controlled his body, his mind, his soul.

The monster rose and spotted a dog not far away. Lacking a collar around its throat, the animal was completely naked, stained with disregard. A neglected stray, the skinny canine was famished; its ribs pushing hard against its grievous hide. It sniffed. Catching the monster's scent, the dog approached. It barked. Overcome by the sight of a potential meal, the dog frothed at the mouth, staring at the monster with charred, feral eyes. The barking quickly made way for a growl. The hound charged. With its mouth wide-open, teeth exposed, saliva slipping off the tips, it leapt. Its fangs clamped down on the monster's raised left arm. The animal's teeth tore through his clothing, its saliva soaking his skin, its warm breath huffing against it.

Seething with pain, the monster flailed his arm, and shook the dog loose. The animal fell to the ground, but quickly collected itself, and lunged again. This time, with both of his hands, the monster caught the hound by the throat.

He squeezed. The dog cried out, its body thrashing violently. Its paws swung like the sharpened curve at the end of a *kusarigama*, but as his grip tightened, and the sound of crunching bones grew louder, the cries turned to helpless yelps. The animal's frantic gesticulations slowed. Amidst these pitiful pleas for mercy, the monster's grip continued to tighten until no air was allowed to enter the suffering animal's lungs. The only sound coming from the dog was the shuffling of its extremities, as it fought for the last seconds of its life. A moment later, the animal went limp.

The monster dropped the dog to the ground and stared at it. The hound's chest rose and fell, for there was a little breath left. He felt no anger, nor sympathy toward the animal. He felt no hatred, nor empathy. He felt nothing at all.

The monster's screaming appetite forced him to kneel down. Empty, guided by a need to feed, he grabbed a handful of the dog's ragged hide and ripped it off, exposing the animal's greasy ribs. The dog bellowed out a tortured howl. The scent of the blood spilling to the ground was seductive. The dog's head whipped around, allowing him to glimpse the animal's eyes as they rolled back in pure shock.

He plunged his hands into the dog's body. The animal let out a final yelp, followed by a thin stream of vomit. He splayed the canine's ribs with a crack. He pulled out a chunk of warm flesh, and shoved it into his mouth, his hunger calming as he chewed and swallowed. Blood spilled from the monster's mouth, covering his clothing with a seal of death.

Despite the ample portions ingested, the monster succumbed to frenzy, and drove his face into the animal's corpse. The dog's meat was tough, tasted horrible, and proved satisfying in the basest of ways, like filthy water gulped in desperation. Soon there was nothing left of the animal but torn ribbons of fur and bones gnawed with tooth marks. The monster slapped his face with both of his hands, and licked his fingers as they prodded his visage. He savored the sweet taste wrapped around each soiled digit. He licked his lips, frantically trying to bask in whatever drop of blood remained. When there was nothing left, the monster began to walk as if his body was teaching itself how; every movement new, reborn.

Surrounding the monster were lush, towering trees, and applauding bushes that swayed from side to side in the breaths of gentle morning winds that lulled with serenity. Simple yet full in all it encompassed, from the blanket of lime green grass that tickled the bottom of his bare feet, to the soft, brown patches of earth cushioning the impact of each step, there was an absence, an aloofness, as if nature, despite its visibility, was withdrawing from itself, terrified of encountering the monster, forcing it to leave behind everything but its own reflection.

The monster turned and spotted a path beyond to where the sky appeared much darker. He took a single step on the path, but the trail was uneven. With his next step, the monster stumbled on a thick root protruding from the ground, felt a crack, heard a pop, and collapsed. With his clothing ripped and torn the fresh morning air pelted his exposed skin, infuriating a collection of wounds scattered over his chest and thighs. After several agonizing moments lying on the ground, he managed to stand up again, but was forced to put all of his weight on his left foot, as the bone just above the right had shattered. He let out a tormented groan.

The monster wanted to stop and to lie back down on the ground in hopes of silencing his suffering, but his body rebuked the notion. His hunger demanded he continue. No longer walking, he hobbled in a disjointed shuffle, the intensity of the pain growing with every movement, dizzying his senses, driving everything else from his consciousness. He dragged his ruined foot like an iron ball at the end of a chain.

In the silence of the path, the monster's appetite roared. He pushed on. His jaw gaped open, sucking in as much air as possible, a poor substitution for the flesh he craved.

With the concept of time governed by the gusts of wind swirling throughout the air around him, he had no idea how long he'd travelled, or how far.

When he reached the point on the path where the sky above him went dismal, where darkness entwined with light, an unyielding dreariness overcame him. The fresh smell that had filled the monster's nostrils upon his awakening was swept away by the sludgy scent of desolation that fell from the sickly heavens above.

The green trees that had encircled him earlier were gone. The ground beneath his callused feet hardened. He was no longer walking on a path of soft earth, but rough pavement.

He stumbled along the road as a morsel of food tunnels through the throat of a body lay flat on a stone slab. As far as his wan eyes could see, there were three unending rows of cars, all tightly squeezed against each other, bumper to bumper, motionless, their lifeless headlights staring at him blankly.

Again, the scent of his surroundings shifted, as a breath of strange air accosted him. There had been food where he stood, but not anymore.

The monster listened, hoping to catch a trace of life he hoped would satisfy his hankering, but he heard nothing. The pain in his ruined ankle had numbed, his body accepting its burden, and embracing the agony it knew would never end. He continued down the road, glancing into cars he passed, hoping to find some food, but every automobile was vacant, devoid of anything.

The pit of his stomach yearned for nourishment just as a baby yearns for life, crowning. Desperate, he moaned, hoping it would scare up something. He had walked long enough on the pavement that large, grey buildings came to crowd him from every side, casting enormous, murky silhouettes that stifled the sun's fading vision, preventing it from seeing the horrors below their shadows. The faces of the buildings bore countless windows, some open and some closed, like a cluster of blinking eyes.

With his crippled ankle killing any notion of moving at anything beyond a slow walk, and his hunger pangs driving him mad, the monster considered stopping, giving up, but was driven onward by an uncontrollable, primal urge. At this point any connection between his body and his mind had been severed. He was a prisoner trapped in a cell with walls of skin and bars of bone. There was no escape from the single-minded purpose of the vessel that enslaved him.

And so he continued to move forward, passing car after car, all pointed in the opposite direction to where he was headed, until he could go no further.

Standing before him was what appeared to be an insurmountable wall of cars that together rose like a wave of twisted metal, smashed plastic, shattered glass, and torn rubber.

Desperately trying to find a way through the blockade of tangible panic and fear, the monster was guided solely by the hunger that demanded he cross the barrier separating the past from the present.

Painfully maneuvering through the wall of steel, he miraculously found a thin seam of space that connected through to the other side. With painful contorting, he managed to make his way through the wall. On the other side, the surroundings changed drastically.

The first thing he noticed were fliers spread out everywhere, thousands littering the ground like dead leaves in a barren forest; all of them stained by the trampling of shoe and boot prints. Each piece of paper bore a blackened photo of a different person. Despite the dreary surroundings, every face in the pictures flashed a knowing smile, as if they reveled in the satisfaction of being there only in print. The monster knelt down and looked at one of the photos before grasping it with his filthy fingertips. He was charged by an urge to eat the owner of the plump face smiling back at him.

Huge fires surrounded him like a captivated audience; their crackling laughter shattering the spell of starvation bounding him with manacles of a promised meal. He rose and stared at several piles of charred corpses. The burning cadavers breathed deeply and flared out in magnificent displays of burning light, unleashing puffs of thick black smoke that rose from the piles of burning tissue. Fixated on one such fire, the monster's eyes were hypnotized by the glow of its cresting flames. Drawn to it, he approached, slowly dragging his useless foot behind him. As he got closer -- the fire's heat singeing his exposed skin -- his body revolted and backed away. At a distance where the flames' sweltering ire could not be felt, he continued staring at the fire, entranced by its constant state of change. The smell of the cooking flesh was enticing, but the fangs of flame denied him satisfaction.

He looked around, surveying, smelling, starving, but could find no food. As his stomach growled, the monster suddenly caught an alluring scent. He peered down to his feet. The pavement beneath him was stained with streaks the color of rust. He knelt down. The brief movement was horrendously painful. Balancing himself on his good foot, he lowered his head, and sniffed a thin sheet of dried blood that was spread around him like a nimbus of anguish. Abandoning his balance, he fell flat to the ground. The monster began to lick the claret stain, slowly, seductively running the surface of his tongue along its surface, as his arms were spread, his palms resting on the delicious nectar. Though it did little in the way of nourishing him, the taste was narcotic. He continued licking the ground like a starving dog, lapping up as much as he could. He only stopped when the pavement had regained its original dull, grey luster.

He caught a glimpse of something moving. Not wishing to startle the potential prey, the monster slowly pulled his arms close to his body and carefully pushed his chest up, as his legs, matching the fragile speed of his arms, also moved into a crouch. Unable to make out the figure moving from one side to the next, he stood slowly, and began to creep toward the source of the movement. As he got closer, the monster's hunger intensified. He saw the figure move again, only this time he was able to identify it as a human.

Fat and lumbering, the human didn't appear to notice the monster at first, but after a brief pause, and a clear confirmation of what hunched before it, the human unleashed a hysterical scream before fleeing in terror. The monster followed, and despite the injury to his ankle, he gained ground quickly. Fearfully wailing, the running human collided with whatever objects lay in its path.

With the distance between them lessening by the second, the monster could see the human's fear, as it turned its head around revealing a pair of plump red cheeks that inflated and deflated with panicked, strained breaths.

Summoning one last rush of energy, the human managed to widen the distance. The valiant attempt did not pay off. Exhausted, the human's flaccid eyes failed to see a pole at the end of the street, a dented stop sign perched atop. After crashing into the slender obstruction, the human fell to the ground, and lay on the pavement motionless.

Closing in, the monster raised both of his arms. His fingers wiggled, their tips aching to grasp and tear at what lay ahead.

Standing over his prey, the monster saw a large gash in the center of the human's forehead. Watching blood spurt out of the human's head drove him into mindless lust.

The fat human huffed incomprehensible noise, as the monster motioned toward its abundant belly that rose and fell with every breath.

As he got closer, the smell and sight of his prey's ample, tender meat aroused him, filling his body with the warmth of ravenous bliss.

Suddenly the human rolled onto its side, gasping; it attempted to roll yet again, halting halfway, desperately gripping the pavement with its palm. Frantic, the human snapped a bone in its hand. The sound was so clear the monster was able to hear it even amidst the human's bawls of pain. Not wanting to risk his prey's possible escape, the monster quickly thrust both of his hands against the human's shoulders, pushed its back flat on the ground, and leaned down.

"Oh God, oh God! No, *please*, God don't let this disgusting animal, *please*, God, *no*!"

The dying meal threw its arms up in an attempt to hold him off, but the strength behind the human's appendages was sapped, in large part to the blood gushing from the wound in its head. Still the human persisted in its desperate fight to live. The monster stared into the human's eyes; they were dilated. Weakness permeated throughout the human's body, yet it continued to struggle.

The monster lowered his head even more; his mouth was close enough to touch the human's chubby cheeks with his tongue.

The monster felt a punch land squarely on his jaw, stunning him. As he regained his composure, the monster saw the fat human attempt to push itself upright, but fail in the attempt, as its hands slipped in a puddle of its own blood.

The monster pounced on his prize, grabbed both of the human's shoulders with both of his hands, and leaned down with all his weight, preventing any further, unexpected blows. He opened his mouth wide. Saliva fell from the tips of his teeth just as tears fell from the human's eyes, striking the ground and mixing with the blood pooling on the pavement underneath its body.

He shot his head down toward the human's pulsing throat. As he clenched, tore, chewed, and swallowed a supple sliver of flesh, his prey released a scream so piercing it forced him to abstain from his gorging in favor of covering both of his ears with his hands.

The monster looked down. The human's face was a portrait of uncertainty. The human appeared to not comprehend what was happening, and what was going to happen. So, in a fearful reflex, left with little else to do, the human continued screaming. With the monster's dead weight pressing down on the human's body, there was no escape.

"Please, I'll do anything. People. I'll bring you people. Kids, women, *anything you want*," the human said faintly; its words gurgling as aerated blood bubbled up its throat. "No, don't, pleas--"

With the screaming subsided, substituted with whispered, easily tolerated words, the monster threw his mouth forward, and thrust his teeth deep into his prey's throat. He relished the taste, cutting off the human's final words, silencing them forever.

Choking on the blood that spouted out with such intense pressure he had to pause for breath, the monster caught a glimpse of the human's still opened eyes staring back at him.

He ate, ravenously, mouth frothing and slick. Drooling and snarling, his eyes rolling around like those of a shark.

The meal was quickly finished; it was delicious, plentiful, satisfying, for the meat was joined by mounds of savory fat that soaked his tongue before sloshing down his throat.

After his final bite, painful cramps erupted throughout the monster's chest. Agonizing, the barbs of pain condemned him to a fetal position, where he stayed for several moments. Writhing on the ground, he rolled to the side and faced the remains of his meal. Bones, most of which still had several succulent strands of meat stuck on them, were scattered, encased by a small circle of blackened ichor. He turned away from the crimson pool, refusing to indulge in any more, regardless of the relentless demands of his ravenous desire. He stood, putting all of his weight on his good foot.

The fires continued to burn around the monster, and the intense clouds of smoke expanded and grew in volume, causing his eyes to water, forcing him to move away. His cramps persisted, and every painful step increased their ferocity.

He shuffled down a long, empty road that offered him brief patches of smoothness. The street's surface was filled with cracks and holes, ruptures and fractures. Like a broken foundation, a shattered body, the road had been abused by the elements, and left to crumble without care.

With his cramps reaching their pinnacle, the monster leaned forward and vomited. Small pieces of flesh he had failed to chew in the midst of his zealous consumption spilled from his mouth. They formed a putrid pool on the splintered, pitted street.

Garbage was everywhere, spilling over the tops of several small receptacles that, like the monster, had consumed more than they could contain. The result was a path of refuse so thick he was forced into a precarious dance of constant stopping and starting in an effort to find patches of open road from which he could step. During one such pause, he spotted a half eaten sandwich, roasted meat leaking out from all sides. Curious, he knelt down, picked it up, coughed up whatever chunks of denied flesh festered in his throat, and took a large bite. He immediately spit it out, as the taste of the roasted meat -- in spite of his carnivorous urgings -- was unbearable.

The monster dropped the sandwich on the filthy ground, and in seconds, he saw several large cockroaches that appeared to come out of nowhere convene around it before consuming it. He took a step back as more of the scavenging insects scurried toward the discarded food. He stared for a few moments as the insects went about their business, caring nothing about him, nor the mayhem taking place around them. Despite their heady numbers, they moved without a hint of aggression toward one another, as they graciously corralled the food that fell into their midst.

2.

The monster passed beneath a duo of street lights that dangled from a wire spread from one side of the road to the other. The lights flashed between yellow and red, but he did not yield.

He looked up at the buildings lining both sides of the road. The structures appeared to be abandoned, their doors and windows covered by boards of wood fastened by iron nails. Some of the boards appeared to pull away and despite the nails' best efforts jutted out like crooked teeth. The buildings appeared to lean down, judging him harshly, and like vulgar tattoos, bright neon scribbles of exuberant spray paint covered their derelict skin. The vibrant images were interrupted by crudely pasted white posters that had the words *THE END IS HERE* written on them in tarry red ink. The meaning of the words slipped across the surface of his mind like river water flowing over the face of a submerged stone.

So many traces of life, yet no life to speak of, he walked alone through the shed skin of what was.

He reached a tunnel of concrete that stretched out and canopied the uneven road like an awning of dark foliage. Pinpricks of light in the distance grew as he progressed through the ellipse. He scanned the walls on his right and left, for they were covered by dour, apocalyptic renditions of the vivacious, natural surroundings that greeted him upon his awakening.

Reaching the midway point of the tunnel, he began to slow his already labored pace, for the pavement beneath his feet had grown much worse than before. It began to slope up and down, rising and falling like a furious sea.

Walking beneath a series of lights flickering above his head, he could hear piercing screams from beyond the tunnel's gaping mouth. His hunger grew fiendish, driving him toward the songs of torment. Closer and closer the noise grew louder. Bang after bang after bang rang out in furious succession. The mixture of screams and explosive bursts created a crescendo of chaos. He continued forward, walking along the surface of the tunnel's extended tongue, unfazed, unafraid, until he reached a site of utter pandemonium.

It was a perfect square, wide and expansive, ambitious and grand. It was surrounded by buildings; one of which -- the most imposing of them all -- was the color of ash. It was older than anything else in the square. Each one of the enormous building's sharpened peaks was topped with stone crosses that loomed over everything. A small group of granite angels were spread out along the rooftop, gazing down, each one armed with smiles stretching from cheek to cheek.

On the other side of the square was a long, far reaching edifice adorned with layers of balconies of equal length, all framed with golden rods and festooned with velvet cloth the color of aged blood. On the remaining two sides of the square were pieced together structures that opened up paths to smaller streets as if they were hidden escape routes.

Despite the enormity of the square's framing, the monster's attention was devoted to the center of its canvas. It was filled with people, a portrait of the populace. At first it appeared as if they were congregating harmoniously, but it took mere moments for him to behold the meaning behind their segregation. Divided into factions whose feuds were clear, the square was a powder keg, and he arrived just in time to witness the lighting of its fuse.

One group ran swiftly, screaming hysterically, their image no more than a blur. Another group was populated by motionless men positioning themselves in a tightly formed line, iron gun barrels pointed at a third group of fiends that looked just like the monster. The fiends neither ran, nor stood shoulder to shoulder, but moved placidly. Draped in frayed clothing, blood trickling down the chins of their dark faces, they were indifferent to the screams of those running away from them, or the blasts from the muzzles of the guns, as they were powered, possessed by starvation.

Standing at the entrance to the square that was filled with enough life to feed him a thousand times over the monster's position as a spectator was short lived. The scent, sight, and sound of such an abundance of food forced his body into the melee.

Surprisingly he went unnoticed, allowing him to approach the conflicting groups as they ran from, walked toward, and fired at each other.

When the monster got closer, he fixated on the man standing at the forefront of the motionless men who fired their guns into the pressing horde of fiends.

"Don't stop firing until nothing is left of them," said the man, who appeared to be in charge, a leader, a hero, for his men followed his directions as if by instinct.

Tall, robust, with a head of slicked back, sable hair that swallowed all light around it, the man was dressed in the same navy blue uniform worn by every other member of the armed brigade. Like every man who followed him, the square chested man also had on a pair of large black boots, and a thick, black vest that provided him with a substantial addition of girth. The only difference between his attire, and that worn by the men who followed him, was a burnished gold badge securely placed on his vest, right over his heart.

One of the people who desperately tried to flee the chaotic scene, an old woman, short and fat, after passing behind the hero and his line of armed men, stopped, and confronted the man. She didn't say anything as she fell to her knees and began to kiss the man's right hand. Bowing before him, her puckered lips carefully avoided the metallic skin of the large pistol held firmly within the hero's clenched palm. Appearing not to notice the benediction of the kneeling female, the hero looked on, shouting orders for his men to continue firing, to continue killing all those who moved toward them.

Suddenly the old woman stood, kissed the hero on the cheek, and ran off to the safety behind the wrath of his men. Then, as the firing ceased, another group of people stampeded toward them. A young woman, tall and lean, at the forefront of the group, began to plead to the hero.

"They're right behind us. Please, *help us.*"

The hero took a step to the side, and looked behind the woman, and those who followed her. Seeing that the size of the group of fiends was nearly three times as large as the group he led, the hero raised his firmly gripped pistol, and like the blade of a guillotine after receiving the permission it craves, he dropped it down, and shouted in a voice of tempered steel, "The few for the many! *FIRE!!!*"

With the opening shot supplied by the pistol held in the hero's right hand, staccato gunfire pierced the air, as both groups -- the fiends and those fleeing from them -- were cut down by the bullets of the hero and his men. It was a slaughter, led by a slaughterer of slaughterers and the slaughtered alike.

With nothing but corpses falling before him, the hero raised his left arm. He turned toward the men who followed him, shouting, "Look at those behind you. The ones *we* saved. Forget those behind me, those who were kept beyond the reach of our help, beyond the reach of God himself."

Unexpectedly the hero spun around yet again, pointing his gun directly at the monster, while he stood still gazing lustfully at the feast of fallen bodies. A moment later, accompanied by a wild roar, the hero fired, but instead of falling like so many others who stood before the hero's pistol, the monster was left standing, unharmed, as an unsuspecting fiend inadvertently crossed between him and the line of fire. Struck in the back, the unlucky fiend fell forward, but not before boring his eyes directly into the monster's, revealing an expression of gripping shock.

The monster looked down at the victim of the hero's bullet, and watched as it withered on the ground, seething with grief, rolling from side to side. Despite the dying groans, the monster was pitiless, gazing at the pool of blood quickly circumventing the source of the agonizing ballad. Just as the fiend finally succumbed to the firm grip of death, the monster knelt down and surrendered to the whims of his appetite, sinking his teeth into the neck of the newly deceased.

For this surrender the monster was rewarded with a lancing pain that throttled his entire body. He stood, and spit out the chunk of carrion he tore off the fiend's corpse. He began to heave then vomited. He saw the small bundle of rejected flesh in front of him. He took a staggered step back. His muscles seized as if he were dosed with potent venom.

A moment later, the hairs slipping out of the monster's nostrils began to sting, as a cloud of what smelled like hydrogen sulphide wafted toward him. He backtracked away from the body, whose rotten taste and rancid smell repelled him, but stopped, when he saw the hero approach.

The monster stood his ground, awaiting the arrival of the hero, gazing at his exposed throat. Another large group of fiends that appeared out of nowhere flanked the hero and his men, instantly consuming their attention, forcing them to spin around and fire their weapons, their bullets mowing several of the fiends down.

With the scent of the dead the monster tasted still abusing his senses he fled until he was concealed by the large, dark shadow of a steely blue building looming overhead. He watched the square through his sallow vision, as the last of the fiends were put down by unwavering, mordant blasts of lead.

Afterwards, the hero, joined by two large members of his coterie, approached the dead fiend who had saved the monster's life by absorbing the bullet destined to strike him. They grabbed both of its shoulders, and picked it up. They dragged the fiend toward the hero as he walked toward the center of the square, the surface of which gleamed carmine, as if covered by a sheet of bloodied ice.

Secure in his position of safety, the hero stood in the center of the square in front of a massive pole upon which a giant flag waved mightily, flapping in accordance with the swirling wind it was able to manipulate with an ease that bordered on arrogance.

From the center of the square, the hero spoke. The man's words, while incomprehensible to the monster, appeared to rile up his riotous men, who all pointed their weapons upward and fired at the sighing sky in fits of explosive celebration. The salvo was so intense several of the bullets pierced the flag swaying above. The flag sagged, while the wind, fed up with the immense weight of its thick woven fabric, turned away from the wounded emblem.

The hero looked up at the limp flag, and raised his arm, signaling his men to stop shooting, and restarted his speech in a voice so booming the monster was able to hear the man's words as if he were standing right in front of him, addressing him directly.

Cries erupted from the hero's men. Meanwhile, the monster continued to hide underneath the blanket granted him by the shadow of the building standing tall behind his back. He waited for the hero and his men to leave, so he could finally feast on the boundless buffet offered by the fallen fleeing people, whose blood, he noticed after inhaling deeply, ran clean.

When the men's fervor died down, and the only sound heard was the whispered fluttering of the flaccid flag trembling above, the two large members of the hero's clan dragged the body of the fiend they grabbed earlier toward the center of the square. Each man gripped the fiend's arms so tightly the monster was able to hear the sockets in its shoulders pop.

"I want each and every one of you to look at this unfeeling creature that chose to feed on us," The hero said.

The two large men holding the corpse began to shake it in what appeared to be an effort to reanimate it, to mimic life, causing its head to teeter back and forth like a marionette.

"It feels nothing except the need to feed on you, me, and every single person you care about."

The hero pointed his pistol at the already dead fiend, whose body was propped up by the two men firmly gripping its shoulders, and fired at its kneecap. The fiend didn't make a sound.

"See," the hero said triumphantly. "It feels nothing. Neither should you when you put them down."

The hero then pointed his weapon directly between the eyes of the fiend and pulled the trigger. Immediately afterwards, as the two burly members of the hero's group dropped the corpse to the ground, the hero said loudly, "It doesn't matter if these creatures can't feel anything. All that matters is they can die."

The crowd of men cheered, as the hero paced in a tight circle, reveling in the sound of their approbation. Once stopped, his face flush with glory, the hero continued with his speech.

"I know most of you have lost somebody you care about. I've lost everyone: My wife, my kids, my brother, my sisters, my mother, my father. Everyone." The hero paused, and bowed his head. Sensing the sentimentality on behalf of their leader, the men before him bowed their heads as well, but before the last man's head lowered, the hero's head was already raised.

"I promise each one of you that I will do everything in my power to make sure those who took so much from you, so much from me, are wiped out."

One of the hero's men, much younger than the rest, shouted out, "Sir?"

The young man dressed in the same uniform as the hero paused and shook his head before continuing, "How can you possibly believe we can kill them all? Look around you, look how many of them there are. They outnumber us at least, *at least*, fifty, one-hundred, probably even *a thousand* to one, maybe more."

The hero peered at the young man, "Are you afraid?"

The young man replied, "Sir, of course I'm afraid. It would be insane not to be. These people, or creatures, or things, or whatever you want to call them, want to tear us limb from limb. With all due respect, there is no way you can tell me, or anybody here, that you're not afraid."

The hero looked at the young man with a granite glare, and said, "I'm an educated man, and I'm smart enough to know that it is foolish to fear those I am trained to, designed to, destined to destroy."

The young man tried to respond, but his words were drowned out by a burst of cheers from the mouths of the rest of the men who surrounded him, while the hero, a smile spreading across his face, joyously shouted out, "Now, let's go hunting!"

3.

With the hero in front, leading his followers out of what was now an enormous graveyard, the group of armed men finally moved away. The monster stepped out of the sanctity of the steel building's shadow. Bodies were piled high, their limbs strewn across other carcasses, never to move again, while blood ran in rivers, reflecting the gaze of the rising sun.

With the sun's increased presence came a heat that caused the monster's skin to moisten and itch, as sweat formed and grew thicker with every throbbing step of his ruined right foot.

He approached the bodies deemed safe to feed upon, the bodies of the fleeing people, and paused as he heard a loud hum from above, as if an unseen buzz saw was coming down upon him from the heavens. He looked up, and against the blinding glare of the sun, dousing its presence, was a dark cloud of flies, millions of them, each with a bright orange head that looked like a shrunken pumpkin. The cloud, moving in a dreamlike pattern, quickly covered the entire square. The combined roar of their tiny wings shook the windows of the buildings surrounding the square until they shattered, and showered the ground with jagged shards. It was as if the square itself, unsettled by the sins of the surface, shook with rage and shed crystal tears.

The cloud of flies exploded, as if a stick of dynamite was lit, tossed, and detonated in the center of it, causing the flies to fan out. They covered the bodies blanketing the square like grains of sand in a sprawling beach, while, for the moment, paying him no mind. He watched the flies jump from body to body, not caring whether or not it was fiend or human. They fed on the corpses with such ferocity, such determination, that they effortlessly breached the barrier of their prey's skin and dove into the bones beneath, which they broke through on their way to the marrow inside.

As he got closer to the bodies, he watched the black masses suddenly alight and fly around randomly. Frenzied, the flies moved with crazed recklessness. It became clear they had become infected with the same fanatical hunger the monster knew all too well.

As the monster approached the bodies on the ground, the fiercely buzzing insects bunched together, forming a wall that veiled the sun. Forced to wave his arms in an effort to get through it, the monster was lost, unable to tell one direction from another. Confused, he lost his balance and fell to the ground. When he rolled over onto his back and looked up, he saw the wall of flies bearing down upon him, mistaking him for one of their lifeless meals. They swarmed him, covering his body in a blanket of hellacious darkness. The monster tried to fend them off, but their persistence was rooted in predatory madness. The flapping of their wings deafened him, beating his eardrums, rattling his skull with piercing pain. Flies covered the whole of his body, their weight preventing him from moving, paralyzing him. Suddenly, he heard nothing, as a rush of flies burrowed deep into his ears, silencing their own sound.

Everything went black when a large group of flies zeroed in on the monster's opened eyes, completely covering them while attacking the thin layer of membrane of his retinas. He let out a tortured groan, but his cries were snuffed when the flies rushed inside the pleading orifice of his mouth with such force his airway was abruptly cut off, and he was unable to breathe. Deaf and blind, his mouth filled with flies that bit and chewed their way deeper and deeper down his throat.

Adrenaline granted the monster the power to thrash his arms around. Ignoring the immense weight of the swarm, he was able to plunge a free hand deep into his gaping mouth. He pulled a clump of writhing insects free from his throat and gasped the city's smog filled air. He sat up and struck himself again and again in the face to disturb the clusters of flies covering his throbbing eyes. Successful, he managed to open them. Gone was the jaundiced tint from which everything was viewed since his awakening, replaced by a scarred vision, where everything he saw appeared through a cracked lens. He looked down. His other hand was covered with nibbling flies that cared little as to which part of his body they indulged. He slammed his occupied hand on the ground, killing several of the insects, but crushing his knuckles in the process. He stood, extended his index finger, and shoved it into his ears, first the left, then the right, mining through them, digging out the flies stubbornly resisting inside.

With his senses once again his own, the monster wiped away as many flies from his body as he could, and retreated as quickly as his shattered ankle would allow.

As he fled farther and farther away from the center of the square, where the flies maintained their dominance, and got closer to the empty street from whence he came, the monster was met by another, much different horde, whose members, though far less in numbers when compared to the pumpkin-headed flies, were much larger in size.

They came from everywhere, as if they bled from the bowels of the city itself. From every sewer, every rusted dumpster, every overstuffed garbage can, every crevice within the city's dank, dirty streets, large brown rats stampeded toward the square, their fangs exposed, gleaming, anxious to dig deep into the bodies laying dead under the watch of the murdered flag.

Standing still, the monster stared at the rats, as they came closer and closer. They completely covered the street, turning it into a road of soiled fur and wiry tails. They ran toward him without regard. When they reached him, they, just like the flies before, assumed he was no different than the dead from which they hoped to gorge.

They covered the monster's feet, gnawing on them both, before climbing on top of each other in a scene of grotesque solidarity, as they scaled his legs, biting deep into the skin left exposed by his torn trousers. The bites, larger and more painful than those of the flies, caused him to topple to the ground. Once there, the rats mobbed him. The pain was transcendent, and he expressed it in his screams. The monster rolled over, revealing his back. His cries cut short as he buried his face in the pavement.

With what little life he had left hanging precariously in the balance, the monster pushed himself up into a standing position. Paying no mind to the depleted condition of his body, he lurched over to a nearby staircase and scaled the steps.

He crawled to the top, sat, breathed deep, and watched as the stampeding vermin spilled into the square like a rushing flood of shit. Immediately upon entering, the rats clashed with the flies over the food awarded to the victor.

Exhausted, the monster's stomach seized. He saw flaps of skin hanging from both of his kneecaps exposing patches of brawn and bone. He reached down, grabbed the loose flesh and ripped it off. The pain was intense, but brief. As more rats streamed down the street to reinforce their brethren in their battle with the flies, he inhaled the smell of his own meat before plunging it into his mouth. The satisfying chunk of his own flesh caused him to tear off the other loose patch from his other kneecap. This time he ignored the familiar sting, consuming that piece of meat as well.

The mouthfuls of his own flesh made the monster's hunger roar, and with it, the temptation to continue to tear at his own body. Resisting the urge that caused every single one of his joints to shake and tremble, he stared out at the square where the overwhelming number of rats finally began to assert their dominance. Most of the flies retreated from their spoils. The remaining flies however, refused to yield. Screams of several rats could be heard, as the flies that chose fight over flight swarmed them until nothing of the animals could be seen. The rodents were transfigured into scurrying lumps covered with orange headed insects.

From his hideout above the square the monster watched the skirmish rage on between the two sects of scavengers with each side trying to claim all the carcasses covering the square. Eventually, the winner was proclaimed, as the last of the flies flew away, leaving behind a squalid mischief of rats, who celebrated their victory by feasting on the bodies of the dead.

As destroyers and devourers of the past itself, the vermin tore, chewed, and swallowed it, spitting out memories. What was not consumed by filthy gnashing teeth was left behind to rot. Meanwhile, the sun's rays, due to the disintegration of the cloud of pumpkin-headed flies, once again pierced through the thinning sheets of the smoggy blanket covering the city, and aimed its light at the rats, where its illuminating stare exposed the pure, cerise color of each one of their beady eyes.

The rats had left the monster's already ravaged body in a state of complete ruin; however, with the smell of fresh blood reaching his nostrils at the behest of a sudden gust of wind, his insatiable need to feed gave him the strength required to stand again.

Once erect, the monster stepped down the steps of the small staircase that had saved his life, and walked back down the narrow street toward the square.

With their feral nature spiraling out of control, the rats ignored the abundance of bodies that could provide enough food for each and every one of them several times over. Juvenile rats turned on their mothers, while mothers in turn devoured their young. The largest rats ate any smaller rats that showed any inclination toward their plunder. Packs of small rats began to form. These gangs would corner and murder any large rat they could find. Whether out of jealousy or greed, or simply as a result of their base nature, the entire mob of rats soon turned on each other, ripping each other apart in mindless defense of the food they now disregarded.

Standing at the mouth of the street, the monster caught sight of a body fronting a large contingent of corpses. Barely breathing, but alive enough to be killed, it was brutally injured, but left whole.

As he walked toward the body, the monster caught a glimpse of his own reflection in a large window; a witness with no objections, the pane coldly congratulated him. He swept aside several long strands of disheveled brown hair, revealing the extent of the damage his countenance endured. Coated by grime and gore, he was draped in a scabrous shell. Immune to the little light that leaked through the smoggy sky above, the natural hue of his skin was a mystery. His eyes remained scarred, his lips pallid, colorless. He opened his mouth; his teeth and tongue flashed bright red, enlightened by the consumption of his own flesh. The monster had a face to be feared.

The deafening squeals from the clashing rodents rang out like a macabre orchestra of tortured strings as they continued to destroy each other. The piles of rodent carcasses grew higher than those of the fallen people and fiends they so rabidly rushed to consume. The monster kept a focused eye on the mayhem, while the scent of the body he hoped to devour continued to entice him.

The body belonged to the tall, lean woman who had pleaded for help from the hero and his men, moments before they pointed and fired their weapons at her, those who followed her, and those who pursued them.

Blood leaked from several of the wounds scattered throughout the woman's chest. The smell was euphoric. The monster leaned down, remaining outside of her vision. He paused when he heard the woman start to choke, before spitting out a scarlet geyser. With her senses regained, but her body too ravaged to move, the woman began to wildly move her eyes from right to left, but still did not see him.

Perhaps she was hoping to see a fellow survivor from the group of people she had led to destruction. Perhaps she believed she was in a dream that had started grim and hopeless only to progress to a world of joy and pleasure. Or perhaps she was accepting the pain she felt pummeling her chest as a result of the bullets that had pierced her skin from neck to naval, and wanted to see all she could before expiring.

"I can't move," she screamed. "Somebody please help me. Please, somebody, anybody, *help me*!"

As the woman continued to cry for help that would not come, some of the nearby rats stopped their infighting, and zeroed in on the source of the noise. The monster stood, as hundreds of rats pointed their twitching snouts toward the woman like missiles locked onto a target. Oblivious to the fate she would suffer as a result of her cries for help, the woman continued to try to move her body in hopes of emancipating herself from her position. She was unsuccessful, thwarted by the crippling extent of her injuries.

The rats formed a large circle that encased both the monster and the injured woman. The monster turned his attention to the pack of rats, as they inched closer and closer. They all had twisted faces covered in strands of flesh. Their eyes, which just moments ago had glowed like precious rubies, appeared so overdosed with greed and indulgence they now looked like smeared black pearls devouring the limited light of day. The rats moved sluggishly as their bellies swelled; their bloodied teeth unsheathed like swords.

Looking back at the woman, the monster positioned himself in front of her limited vision, and once there, she let out a shriek.

He looked down at the woman, his eyes focused on the bullet holes spread all over her body, as they continued to spill fresh blood. He then looked toward the rats, who had continued to inch closer. They had just about reached a point where their opportunity to pounce was at hand. If he waited any longer, he would surely lose out on the meal, and so the monster threw out his hands, thrust them down on the woman's shoulders, opened his mouth, and plunged it down upon her throat. She screamed at the initial impact, but it only lasted a moment, as it was abruptly silenced after he rose, chewing, while watching her eyes close.

The rats -- startled at the sight of him eating -- momentarily pulled back but quickly regained their poise, and recommenced their slow approach toward the woman's now lifeless body. Noticing the rats' progress, the monster ate as fast as he could, tearing off portions the size of his hands, and shoveling them into his mouth, swallowing them whole, while his eyes never left the horde of rats that continued to close in on to him.

While he ate, the monster scrutinized the woman's face through his scarred eyes. It was an essay of hopelessness that had instantly grown ashen. Her eyes, which re-opened as a result of several violent jerks during his gorging, rolled back, revealing a chilling pair of milky white spheres decimated by thin streaks of red. With her mouth open, gusts of stale breath spilled out every time he thrust his hands into her chest.

With the rats at his feet, the monster stopped eating, stood, and took a quick step back, followed by another. The rats ignored him, as one by one, they leapt onto the woman's ravaged body. He watched many of them try to tear off the flesh clasped around the woman's exposed bones, but couldn't because their teeth, after so much tearing, gnawing, and chewing, had dulled their overused edges.

A few of the rats, pausing amidst their fervor, stared right at him; their small, black, empty eyes boring directly into him. The monster took several more steps back before turning, but not before catching a final glimpse of the woman he was leaving behind, whose body was reduced to nothing more than a skeletal recollection of the person she once was.

Even though the monster tried to move as fast as his crippled ankle would allow, some of the still hungry rats started chasing him.

In no time, they caught up to him. While the number of rats attacking him paled in comparison to the multitude he managed to fight off a short time earlier, the fight was still strenuous. Many of the rats, energized by their recent feeding, attacked him fervently, hoping to add to their already impressive intake before lethargy was set to take over.

After the final rat fell, suffering a blow that struck it directly in the snout, the monster made his way back down the same narrow street he took to enter the city's cursed square. Berated by exhaustion, he stopped and looked up at the smoggy sky's sorrowful, grey face as it blended perfectly with the ocean of grim, hoary cement that flooded the rest of the city.

4.

The monster felt a warm sensation along the inside of his thighs. He stopped, looked down, and smelled an odd odor. Unsure as to what it was, he knelt down, carefully putting all of his body's weight on his good leg, and saw a dampened, urine stain around the upper thigh area of his despoiled pants. A moment later his stomach began to cramp. He fell to his knees. He waited for the heaving that had flooded his body earlier to take hold. A different sensation seized control however, as his stomach clenched just before his bowels gave out and he shit himself. The smell was similar to the miasma that hung above the square after the battle between the fiends and the hero's men. Bereft of shame, the smell didn't affect him, and after a single step, the waste nestled between the monster's rectum and his befouled slacks slid down his legs and hit the ground with a crude splash.

With his bodily functions completed, the monster continued his walk down the long road ahead of him, leaving the square behind. Buildings lined both sides of the road, closing him in, while funneling a stream of steady, powerful wind that whizzed, swirled, and pelted his skin.

When the road came to its end, he caught a scent of life, of food, like an angler snags a fish. Veering off, the monster found himself inside a labyrinth of larger streets spread out like veins originating from the heart of the city.

While walking down one of the streets offered to him, he saw errand shoes mismatched and strewn, large bags filled to the brim abandoned, and random pieces of clothing left like neglected orphans. Even vacant baby carriages were left toppled over, their white, soft tops stained by the filth of the street. As he progressed, the monster encountered more human detritus, from newspapers to canes, to bi-cycles and cellular phones, all littering the ground, forsaken by their owners, left for dead.

Dragging his destroyed foot through an empty intersection, where pairs of streetlights flickered from yellow to red, back and forth, cautioning nobody, the monster saw several cars all painted in the same two-color scheme of red and gold. Some of them had been abandoned in crooked positions, their doors swung wide open. Others had crashed into poles. Some were even inside buildings, as they had been driven through the structures' glass faces. Liquids, from green to black, spilled from the orifices of the mutilated automobiles.

The heat from the sun's rays grazed his face, warming him, while crusting the blood, sweat, dirt, and grime left pasted over it, forming a thin mask molded from the rigors of the day.

His body felt tired, weary. The walking fatigued him; however, with the feeling of weakness, the hunger, which preyed on his vulner-ability, began to beat its drum ferociously, forcing the monster to heed its thunderous growl.

Again he veered off and found himself walking on a street twice as wide as the one he had walked along earlier. Instead of the two-toned red and gold cars, this larger street was filled with tin-topped green buses, toppled over, their windows smashed in. There were no signs of present life, only past panic.

Ahead the monster spotted a tall marble pillar centering a spher-ical slab with a golden angel adorned in a long flowing robe, perched atop, guarded by a short fence wrapped around its base. The angel's breasts were firm and supple; its feathered wings lavish and outspread. Yet despite its illustrious presentation, the angel's body was rusted, while its haloed head was defaced by large blotches of bird shit that looked like rotten egg yolks.

He walked past the neglected seraph, leaving it behind, cursed to stare down on an empty city, whose condition resembled its own neglect. He continued on until he was presented with an oasis, a vast park of vi-brant green. There were trees with thousands of still leaves hanging com-fortably from their branches, as the wind that had tunneled fiercely be-tween the walls of buildings had been mitigated by the park's open space.

Reaching the center of the park, the monster encountered a giant water fountain, but it was a fountain in name only, as it refused to spurt a single drop of water from any of a manifold of thirsty mouths. As he got closer he could make out the faces of the statuettes populating the fountain's artistic presentation. They were young children, captured in a state of perpetual joy. Their smiles, expertly etched, spread across their bronzed faces. The children were frozen in frolic, as if stuck in a perfectly coordinated photograph. Together they stared up at the figure of a tall man wearing a dog collar. Despite his baldness the man had long locks of hair falling from the back of his head like water cascading down a waterfall. Held firmly in the man's left hand was a thick book tucked to his side. It was clasped shut. His right hand blossomed open, pacifying the joyous youths, while he peered down at them with a smile permanently extended across his face.

The pool beneath the gregarious looking man and the jubilant children was empty, barren. Like the decaying angel resting atop its pillar outside the park, the statues of the children and the man were left to ruin.

As he leaned over the edge of the dehydrated pool, the monster's hunger balked at the lack of progress toward the scent of life that, while faint, still wafted throughout the air. Still, his weariness remained steadfast. The monster took his defiance a step further, and sat atop the edge of the fountain and rested his beleaguered body.

There were no moments of reflection, no sense of calm, no acceptance, and no respite, only the hunger demanding he get up, and keep moving. Resisting, the monster's head began to pound. Dizzy, his whole body felt like lumbering pulp; nonetheless, he finally succumbed to the yearnings of his most determined drive, hopped off the edge of the empty pool, and recommenced his pursuit of the scent of food. His first steps were painful, as his ravaged ankle, numbed and stiffened during his short rest, unleashed its forgotten torment, punishing him for his indolence.

As quickly as he'd entered the park, and settled in its beautiful center, the monster was forced to leave it behind, abandoning its tranquility.

Gusts of wind struck his face, intensifying the rigidity of the filthy mask smearing his profile, and with the winds came a stronger scent of life. Moisture soaked his cracked lips, and like a rancid fuel, the smell of living flesh pushed his battered body faster, dismissing any discomfort. His surroundings continued to change. The faces of the buildings were cleaner, more refined than those he had passed earlier.

Gone was the stream of spray painted letters. Gone was the red writing. Gone was the grime. Gone was the filth. Gone were the piles of refuse vomited by gluttonous garbage cans. Gone were the cockroaches.

Under these new buildings the monster heard a sudden noise, an enraged shout lined with revulsion. He spun to see a man dressed in a crisp black suit. The human was belting out profanities, while pointing and firing a pistol at a pack of fiends, laying each one down with a single shot to the head. Quickly recalling and responding to the familiarly violent sound, the monster ducked, and moved behind a large nearby dumpster. And like a predator sizing up its prey, he watched as the suited man exhibited crooked joy after executing his own prey one by one.

Alone, the man in the suit shot the last of the fiends that committed the crime of approaching him. He tried to fire another shot, but his weapon let out nothing but a loud click. Storing the memory of the futile noise, the monster watched as the man approached the body of his final victim and kicked it several times in the gut with the tip of his pristine, black shoe that despite the blows still managed to glisten. The man then knelt down and spit on the body, cursing the corpse. The gentleman then pulled down his glinting silver zipper, pulled out his penis, and pissed all over the body of the fallen fiend.

After the man tapped the last few drops of urine, he zipped up his pants, and put his gun back in a holster tucked behind a large flap of his black jacket. He raised his voice in a bold cry, "I'm not running like the rest. I'm not scared of you. My father, my father's father, and his father before him built this city."

The monster's body began to tingle and shake as the patience of his appetite vanished, giving way to desperate pleas for satisfaction due to the close proximity of another meal.

The monster moved from behind the dumpster, hugging the wall. Remaining unseen, he progressed slowly, motioning closer and closer to the man with the suit, stalking him, cunningly closing in.

"Let everybody else run, what do they have to lose?" The man declared.

The monster got closer, his hunger growing, as the man continued to speak to nobody. The monster revealed himself from behind the wall that had kept him shielded from the man's vision. The man, seeing him, jumped back and pulled out his pistol. As the human pulled the trigger, the monster didn't move, or even flinch, but stayed where he was, expecting the sound of the click that indicated the emptiness of the clip, which was repeated again and again to the suited man's loath grunting.

The monster approached the man in the suit, who stood his ground, defiant in his stance, gripping the empty pistol in his hand. The man's face twisted with rage: fury over fear.

"Look at you. You're disgusting. Who are you? *What* are you? I bet you don't know your own name. I bet you don't even have a name. Compared to me, you're *nothing*."

The monster continued approaching.

"*Men* like me don't run away from *nothings* like you," the man said, standing his ground, refusing to give an inch.

The monster listened to every word the man in the black suit said, but they were like short breaths that came and went, as he couldn't understand a single word. All he cared about was the sight of the man's bulging throat pressing out of the collar of his buttoned white shirt.

Now within a few steps of the man, and with the monster's mouth forced open to let some of his yearning saliva escape, the man finally began to show signs of understanding what was happening, and took a short step back.

The monster raised both of his arms and pointed his hands at the man, his fingers wiggling. He let out a groan. He didn't groan to express any specific thought. He didn't even make the sound voluntarily, but as the distance between him and his meal shrank, he groaned in anticipation of being fed.

Within the monster's reach, the man jumped back, as his fear finally caught up with his supreme confidence in the world's ability to keep him insulated from its dangers. The man raised his empty pistol and pointed it directly at the monster.

"You'll never touch me," he said.

The man's hand, clutching the firearm, began to shake, the pistol nearly falling from his grasp. Sweat formed on his forehead. Tiny drops of moisture sprouting up on his brow, rolling down his nose and cheeks.

They both stared at each other silently until their quiet was interrupted by the roaring of the monster's stomach. The monster took a step forward. The man raised the gun higher. The monster hesitated and cocked his head to the side, but the sight of the food overcame any notions of caution, and as he came closer, the human slammed the pistol down like a hammer, striking the monster on the head.

Blood flowed from where the monster was struck. It streamed down his forehead, and fell from the tips of his tangled brown hair. He wiped it away with both of his hands, eliminating some of the gaunt mask of grime covering his face. He licked his fingers, savoring the sweet taste.

Focusing his strength and weight on his good foot, the monster lunged at the man, who was too slow to react to the aggressive counterstrike. The gun fell from the man's hand and hit the ground with a loud clank. The man, still managing to maintain balance after the attack, shouted out, "Come on," through a shrill voice that betrayed the strength he was desperately trying to project.

The monster lunged again. He grabbed the man's hand, where the gun used to be, and squeezed it with every ounce of strength he had left. He pulled hard and tore the man's arm right out of the socket, taking with it the sleeves of both the man's black jacket and his white shirt, staining his suit a gruesome shade of red. The human cried out, shaking the large windows of the ambivalent building quietly watching the scene unfold.

Blood from the socket sprayed the monster, covering his filthy body. He turned toward the man who stared back at him with horror, and wiped his hand across his chest. The monster shoved his hand, covered in blood, deep into his mouth, where he sucked on each finger, swallowing every drop.

The human staggered back; miraculously staying upright, he spun around spraying everything around him. Shreds of loose skin and frayed fabric from his torn shirt and jacket hung from the stump where his right arm used to be. The building behind him, the garbage can beside him, a bench in front of him, everything was stained with red. Blood even reached the pile of corpses the man had dispatched, and for a fleeting moment, despite the death plaguing them, several of the fiends appeared to momentarily reanimate, for they swallowed the precious drops granted them before returning to their previous states of mortis.

Holding the appendage, the monster tore off the fabric sleeve like the wrapper of a candy bar and took a large bite, removing a chunk of the man's bicep. The meat was succulent. He took another, and then another large bite, gorging on the arm until there was little left but greasy bone, torn tendons, and loose pieces of brittle cartilage. Still he wanted more, for a single arm was not enough to satisfy him. He dropped the ragged limb to the ground with a thud, and turned toward the man, who was now on the ground, head down, eyes earthward. A large ruby pool formed around him, its sheen accentuated by a rush of sunlight that burst through the smog above, allowing him to see his reflection up close. Death was near.

The monster approached his fallen victim, yearning to eat more. But before reaching his waning prey, the man held up the only hand he had left, and with eyes filled with disgust, he said, "You may have killed me, but how many of you have I killed? Do you think those bodies over there are the only ones? I've been killing your kind for days."

The monster took another step forward, his head tilted indifferently to the side.

"You think like you're better than me, don't you? You think you've actually beaten me, don't you?" the man asked.

The monster didn't think about anything except his hunger. He took another step toward the man, dragging his bad ankle behind him, his attention focused on the loose flesh dangling from the man's empty arm socket.

With resentment fueling him, the man managed to unclasp the gleaming gold watch wrapped around his wrist, grasped it in his palm, and threw it at his attacker's head. The impact of the watch, though slightly painful, was nothing more than an annoyance, a blip in the monster's progress toward his prey. The man then slipped a glistening gold ring off his finger, squeezed it tight within the clenches of his palm, and threw it as well, striking the monster in the head, and just as before, it did nothing to slow his momentum.

The man dug his only hand into his pant pocket, and pulling a handful of coins onto the ground, he threw them one by one, striking the monster in the face. The coins elicited no reaction. The man then reached around into his back pant pocket and pulled out a smooth, black wallet. He opened it up, and managed to pull out several plastic cards, from blue, to red, to white, to green, and one by one he threw them, but the cards merely bounced off the monster's chest.

When there were no more cards left to throw, the man pulled out a wad of cash. He tossed the bills at the monster, but a sudden gust of wind swept them up and fluttered them through the air before they landed on and drowned in the pool of the man's own blood causing it to ripple ever so slightly. The human then threw the wallet itself, but missed, as his coordination had finally failed him.

The monster continued to close the gap between himself and his prey, knowing it would soon be within his grasp.

The man's movements, reduced to panicked squirming, were a moment later, with fear reaching its apex, so weakened that his entire body went limp. Having been only able to roll onto his back, the human's eyes rolled up and watched the monster close in. In a last gasp of energy, the man kicked out his feet, and managed to loosen one of his shoes. It flew in the air and struck the monster in the shoulder as he continued toward him, undeterred.

The back of the man's head sank down and fell to the pavement with a faint thud, as he could only look up at the emotionless, grey sky above, thin strands of light peeking through.

"You're nothing—"

The monster grabbed the man's neck with his hands, and tore off a ragged strip of skin, silencing the man's antipathy forever.

With his ankle in agony as a result of his pursuit, the monster collapsed willingly atop his prey. Chest to chest, he raised himself to rip open the man's white shirt with both of his hands. The ferocity with which he tore the shirt caused the buttons to pop out, one of which struck him directly in the eye, adding to his already scraped stare. The monster thrust both of his hands into the man's chest, grabbed a rib with each hand, and jerked them up, opening the chest cavity like an eager child opening an extravagant present.

Straddling the dead man like a lover ready and willing to offer the greatest pleasure, the monster held up each rib, and sucked them dry. When done, he tossed them away like the garbage he waded through earlier in the day. He began to eat, plunging his face into the man's opened chest, where he tore, chewed, and swallowed as much as he could, while his belly swelled with ecstasy.

When there was nothing left of the man but a ruined suit soaked with blood, the monster picked up, and sucked on the drenched garments like a child teething on a salty seatbelt.

Sated, the monster let out a mighty belch and vomited, having again consumed more than his body could handle. He looked at the small pool of bile, blood, and chewed chunks of flesh spread before him, knelt down, and consumed it again. His indulgence caused his chest to heave, but this time, resisting the urge to exile the already banished, he managed to keep the food in with the help of another loud belch.

With his appetite slaked, the monster's mind was clear. For a few fleeting moments his hunger's obsession had disappeared, leaving him feeling lost, disoriented, empty. His hunger, the whip that cracked against his back and drove him, had also proven itself to be the one thing keeping him from slumping down on the ground and staying where he was until death relieved him.

5.

The day was dying. The smog above darkened, extinguishing the sun's narrow rays. Traces of a brilliant orange hue comforted the hazy veil the heavens wore like a fresh bride.

The monster stood, and stared down at a long, dark silhouette stretched out beyond his feet. With his shattered ankle seizing, he walked, taking his bleak image with him.

As time swept away the embers from the fires burning within the city's core, he became aimless. He walked down an empty street. The road was lined with monuments of abandonment, vacant cars, their doors swung open, discarded items everywhere -- crushed beer cans, cracked noodle cups, torn receipts, and unwrapped portions of rotten food, half eaten. He had no motivation to examine his surroundings. He was left with nothing to do but stare at the ground as he soaked in the pure, absolute silence save for the breaths of wind that swept down the empty street like a surveying spirit.

Suddenly he caught a scent. He stopped. His stomach convulsed and contracted. He turned. Facing the monster were sharp spikes protruding from a large wrought iron gate. The gate was closed, a thick wall bounding each side, spread around a large open area, embracing it protectively. He approached the gate, searching for the source of the scent that aroused him. It was small, but it was there, a splash of dried up blood on the tip of one of the gate's spikes. He fell to his knees. His tongue unraveled out of his mouth. He pushed his face forward, until the end of the throbbing muscle touched the tip of the spike. He tasted the sweet flavor. Eager for more, he licked the spike aggressively. It pierced his tongue, and he found himself tasting then gulping his own blood. He continued to thrust his face forward until the gate abruptly opened.

The pasture beyond the black gate was unlike anything he'd seen throughout his trek in the ruined city. It was a pocket of oxygen in a thick mist of smoke, a paradise within a desert of destruction.

The monster closed his mouth, sucking his punctured palate so intensely that his cheeks caved in. He glanced to the left and saw a small office with the word *Security* written on the window. He leaned toward the pane of glass. The office was empty, and like many of the streets he travelled, it was abandoned in the wake of evacuated life. He looked up at the top of the wall that stretched out from both sides of the gate and saw twirled strips of razor wire bundled atop its surface like vines overgrowing ancient ruins.

Suddenly, from inside the isolated area, past the gate, a loud smashing sound shattered the silence. A moment later the smashing sound was repeated. The monster passed through the now-opened entrance.

Inside, the monster found what could only be described as a haven. It was spacious, granting him room enough to breathe. It smelled different, as the aroma of freshly cut grass filled his nostrils. The ground beneath his feet felt different, as the ruptured pavement of the streets he grew accustomed to walking upon were replaced by cobblestones that, while uneven, were smooth to the touch. Even the sky looked different. It appeared vast, limitless, managing to quell the quilt of smog covering the rest of the city. Gusts of fresh air breathed down upon him, but not in the same swirling, aggressive pattern from within the labyrinthine city; instead, they flowed in soft waves that brushed against the patches of skin exposed by the rents in his tattered clothing.

Hearing the loud smashing sound just ahead, the monster moved forward. The balls of his feet slid on the surface of the cobblestones. He heard another smash from the same place. Despite the protest from his mangled ankle, he increased his speed.

During his pursuit of the sound that provoked his appetite, forcing his body into the dedicated movement, the monster passed the backs of several houses lining both sides of the wide road. The houses were all identical, each one with a small yard encased by identical fences.

"What's going on in there?"

The words were addressed to a broken window of one of the houses by a man standing on the small patch of grass laid out before it. After asking his question, the man turned around, revealing an infant cradled in his arms, wrapped in a bright red blanket.

"Nothing dad. It was just a few dishes," a voice, young and nasal, said from inside the house.

"Did you find any food?" the father asked.

"No, no food," said a boy, crawling out of the broken window.

The monster continued to get closer.

"That's okay, son," the father said. "Let's check the next house. I know that no one is home. They have a cousin, or an uncle, I can't remember which, who is political. They got the word early. They got out weeks before everything went to hell."

After the boy pulled himself through the broken window, the father turned, catching the monster's eye, and stared at him with an expression of horror that obscured the man's eyes like a thick blindfold.

The father clutched the baby close and grabbed the hand of the young boy, pulling him toward him. The father's knuckles glowed white as his grip tightened around the blanket wrapped infant and the hand of his son.

"Please," the father said. "We're just like you. We're just trying to find food. There are people everywhere, hiding. Go after them, but spare us."

The monster took a step toward the family, replying to the father's pleas with a grunt as his ravaged ankle, caught in a crevice, caused a sharp pain to shoot up his leg.

The father followed the monster's advancing step with a retreating step of his own, while still begging for his life, and the lives of his children.

"I'll show you where the other families are hiding. I will even break into their houses and open their doors so you can get to them. Just spare my family," the father said, his words cracking like his ashen knuckles that gripped his children tighter and tighter.

The monster continued his approach without charge or pause as the father continued his backpedal, both his children in tow. The monster was close enough now to see tears falling deliberately from the father's eyes.

"Why us?" The father shouted. "What did we do to *you?*"

The monster licked his lips, and as his tongue brushed against his teeth, a soft scab from his wounded palette slid free. The taste of his own blood excited him.

The son abruptly grabbed his father's leg with both of his hands, thrusting his face into his father's hip, forcing the man to take an unexpected step to the side, where he tripped on a small stone sitting innocently in the center of the yard. It was a small, insignificant rock that yielded an infinitely larger, catastrophic result, for the infant slipped out of the father's grasp and hit the ground with a thud followed by a shriek of silence.

The father looked down in horror as the infant lay on the grassy ground, exposed; its bright red blanket thrown open like a flower in bloom.

Frozen with shock, the father stayed where he was, his mouth ajar, not permitting a single word to escape. The baby's soft skin glowed under the orange sheet of the sun draped in the sky above.

The sight of the baby's delicate skin thrust the monster into a state his body dutifully obeyed. He lunged toward the infant.

The father shook his son off his leg, the boy fell to the wayside where he landed with a smack and looked up confused.

The monster reached the helpless infant, picked it up, and stared into its plump face. The baby's eyes slowly opened, revealing a pair of perfectly round, moist brown eyes that stared back at him with a profound sense of curiosity.

"Let go of her," the father said taking a determined step forward.

Pulling the baby up close, the monster opened his mouth, wide, anticipating yet another meal. Just as the baby's chubby arm began to enter his mouth, the father let out a wild roar that startled the monster enough to almost allow the squirming infant to slip out of his grasp.

The father did not advance however; instead, he gazed down at his son, who gripped his leg, crying and begging for the life of his sibling.

Faced with a choice, an impossible decision, more tears spilled out of the father's eyes. Unlike before, they were not deliberate, but fell like a torrential rainfall, showing no end in sight, a rainfall that caused floods and forced people to flee from their homes.

The father took a step back. His son released his grip from around his father's leg, and asked, "Why are you walked away? We have to save my sister, save her Dad, *save her*!"

The father said nothing, as he stared at his infant daughter, who started to cry, sensing the danger of the stranger holding her. The father then took a longer step back, and turned toward the cobblestone road that led to the exit of the haven, but his young son stood his ground, "How could you leave her behind? How could you leave her in that monster's hands? He's going to kill her and you're not going to do anything about it?"

The father turned his attention toward his son, "If I attack that monster and lose, what will happen to you? She is already dead son. I've lost one child. I'm not going to lose both."

"You're a liar." the boy said, "You don't care about saving her. You don't care about saving me. You only care about saving yourself."

The father's body shook so violently it seemed as if it was going to explode. Veins from the father's sweat soaked forehead began to pulsate.

The monster looked back at the infant, and once again opened his mouth, and began to insert the baby's arm inside, and as he did so, the young boy rushed toward him.

"STOP!" the father shouted as his son didn't slow, didn't stop.

Charging for the sake of his young sister whose hand was already moistened by the saliva dripping from the monster's teeth, the boy rushed forward like a bull riled up by the taunts of a matador.

Spotting the small boy rushing toward him the monster quickly shoved the whole of the infant's arm into his mouth, warming it with his pungent breath, before clamping his jaws together. There was a scream, so high pitched, so piercing, his eyes squinted, the nerves in the roots of his teeth seizing. The monster jerked his head back, tearing the infant's arm off, hearing a cracking sound as the infant's jaw stretched beyond its physical capabilities, allowing the volume of its screams to increase even more, forcing his eyes shut. He chewed only twice to soften the already tender, delectable meat, before swallowing the infant's chubby arm.

The monster opened his scarred eyes and saw the small boy, an arm's length away, frozen in place, as if stuck in a pool of tar. The boy's face was empty, resembling his own. The boy's arms were hanging straight down, limp, pulled to the ground by the forces of despair. Tears rolled down the boy's cheeks.

Seconds later, the boy snapped out of his state of grief; his eyes coming to life. Blazing with rage, the boy's hands squeezed into stark knuckled fists. The boy raised his clenched hands, wielding them as if they were lethal weapons.

The monster bit and tore off a large chunk of the baby's throat, silencing the infant. He tossed the tiny carcass to the ground, giving him enough time to catch and grab the throat of the young boy who leapt at him maniacally. With his hands wrapped around the boy's neck, the monster looked into the boy's eyes: there was only fury. The boy thrashed his arms and legs, trying to strike him. The monster began to squeeze. Hearing the crunching of the boy's vertebrae buckling under the pressure of his tightening grip, all the anger held captive within the white of the boy's eyes quickly drained, making way for unbridled fear.

As the boy's struggles grew weaker, the monster looked beyond, and saw the father approaching him, sluggishly, as if one of the man's ankles had sustained a gruesome injury similar to his own.

He inhaled deeply before thrusting his head down, and sinking his teeth into the boy's throat. As the monster tore the flesh from the boy's neck, his ears were stung by the tortured wailing of the father, who fell to his knees, pleading at the sky.

The monster's body, fuelled by the two youthful, tender carcasses, began to tremble with pleasure, as he tossed the boy's body aside, where it struck the corpse of the infant. The blood from the small bodies formed a small pool that seeped into the green surface of the yard in front of the house the family had just broken into in search of food.

Turning his back on the grieving father, who he had every intention of consuming shortly, the monster made his way toward the mutilated children. He knelt down, and licked the blades of grass, carefully suckling each one, thoroughly enjoying the sweet taste as if they were soaked with a fine red wine. The monster then moved on to the infant's carcass, which he consumed rapidly, sawing through the skin, flesh, fibers, and tendons with his teeth. After spitting out several small bones, he moved on to the body of the boy.

The monster dove his face into the boy's chest cavity and gorged. He paused, hearing the father stirring behind him. The monster raised his head, turned, and with his face completely covered with the expired life of the father's children, he stared at the man, who was now standing, staring back, with a face teeming with rage. With the whole of the infant's body, and half the boy's churning in his stomach, the monster's hunger nonetheless roared for more, quickly reaching a fevered pitch. He looked at the father, examining the amount of meat clinging to the man's bones. He licked and smacked his lips, stood, and took a step toward the man whose facial expression, like his son's before, abruptly changed, and filled with fear.

The father took a step back, looked at what was left of his young children with a pair of eyes that appeared more scarred than the monster's, and whispered, "I'm sorry," before turning his back, and running away.

The monster took a series of steps toward the rapidly escaping meal, but the father was soon out of sight, leaving nothing behind but the sound of his shoes slapping the surface of the cobblestone road.

The monster returned to the body of the boy, and knelt down, ready to finish his meal, when he saw a small orange dot hovering over the carcass before settling atop a piece of bone near the boy's arm. He recognized the dot as the head of one of the pumpkin-headed orange flies he'd encountered in the city's square, but before he could scrutinize it further, the fly disappeared into the body. Like a leech lurking in the depths of a swamp, the fly attached itself to the base of the boy's arm bone, and began to feed on the marrow inside.

Soon, a small cluster of orange headed flies swooped in. With their focus on the remains of the children's bodies, the flies granted him mercy, which after the vivid recollections of the havoc they had caused him earlier in the day, the monster eagerly accepted.

He finished chewing the last chunk of meat in his mouth, swallowed it, and made his way back toward the haven's opened gate.

The sky's orange hue was replaced by a plush pink that clung to the roaming clouds of smog hovering overhead.

6.

The monster walked the surface of an open street. It was much different from the narrow, cramped corridors he passed through earlier in the day. It was quiet and orderly, defiant, immune to the chaos taking place outside of the path it provided. It was wider, cleaner, and while there were abandoned cars, they did not give off the same disorganized, panicked aura of the vehicles he saw before. They were well behaved, gently caressing the curbs lining the road. He passed the vehicles, all of which gleamed under the illuminating ginger glow of street lamps steadfast in their dutiful watch, while several green power boxes hummed quietly, as if performing a prayer of power.

On both sides of the street the monster saw several roofs, but no homes underneath, for the houses from which the splendid crowns heavily rested were mysteriously shrouded, hidden from view, protected by high reaching, pristine walls equipped with thin wires that looked like baited strands of dragging fishing line.

In the blink of a bloodshot eye, the sky's plush pink tint gave way to a ruby red sheen, before fading to the abysmal blue of dusk. The arcane light of stars could now be seen shining down, while the moon, comfortably curled in a crescent position, glowed regally in the center of the melancholic sky, inspecting all beneath its bright white glare, taking over for a sun that had seen enough.

The monster's eyes lowered back to the street that stretched as far as he could see. Far ahead he saw specks of light far up, littering a silhouette of what appeared to be a mountain at the end of the yellow lit road. Atop the mountain, perched like a diadem, was an exquisite golden light, a beacon, bright and true. It hypnotized him and in an instant, the light pulled him toward it with its luminous persuasion.

With his focus fixed on the glimmering zenith atop the dark mountain, he continued down the road. He passed a row of restaurants, their windows large and grand. Their immaculate interiors looking so presentable despite the chaos digging its nails deep into the city, it wouldn't have been shocking to see a group of well-dressed people, prim and proper, chatty and jovial, enjoying a delectable meal of thick tomato soup and glazed legs of lamb on a bed of soil brown rice, accompanied by slender flutes of rich Brandywine.

As he continued, the enticing scent of life abruptly invaded the monster's nose, accompanied by another stronger odor that stung his nostrils. He let out a grunt and a low groan, hoping the source of the smell would reveal itself amidst the street that continued to appear as if it was frozen in a better time, but nothing came into view, until he saw the figure of a man balancing himself on the outskirts of a shadow cast by a bent streetlamp. The still man said nothing as the monster approached, his scent growing more potent the closer he came. The man was wearing a tattered ensemble so full of rips, holes, and frayed strands of fabric the outfit resembled the monster's own ragged clothing.

The monster continued to approach the ratty-looking man, yet the man stayed still, not even raising his head. The man preferred his state of complete insulation, one that ignored everything around him, in favor of what was playing out inside his own mind.

The man began to stir, moving his body erratically while keeping his head down. Incomprehensible words spilled out of the man's mouth in slurred speech, as if they were being spit out. The lurking scent grew so intense it scorched the tips of the hairs leaking out of the monster's nose.

A loud swishing, like the ocean's waves cresting against a wall of bluffs emerged from a bottle held in the man's hand, which had been covered by the cuff of his oversized, grimy brown coat.

The monster took another step forward. The man looked up, revealing a dark, haggard countenance. Badly tanned, the man's face was full of deep, canyoned wrinkles. The man's eyes looked like small pools of expired milk, reddened by thin veins of intoxication. His crusted lips pulled tight and expelled a slimy white concoction built up in the corners of his cankerous mouth. The man's hair, shaggy and grey, was darkened by several streaking stains as if his head had been dipped into an open drum of petrol.

"What do *you* want?" the man said in an embittered tone of familiarity, as if he were speaking to somebody he'd known all of his life. "Are you here to kick me off this street, too? *This* street, *that* street? What does it matter *what* street I decide to sit on, lay on, and sleep on? The entire city has gone down the toilet, who cares if I decide to find one of the few clean patches of porcelain left?"

Every word the man said was soaked with alcohol, like torn pieces of cloth placed in a condemned building and lit ablaze.

The man straightened himself into an upright position, revealing the bottle held firmly in his hand, as well as the black, elongated nails sprouting from his fingertips like animal claws. The bottle itself was clear, but inside there was a muddy brown liquid that blended perfectly with the smeared colors of the man's emaciated jacket.

The man, who could be called elderly by some, cleared his throat loudly before spitting out a chunk of phlegm that landed on top of the monster's bare foot with a clumpy splash.

The man moved sluggishly, attempting to stand in a gauche, callow manner, but aborted any attempt, as he staggered and shook, before collapsing half-way up, and falling back down onto the curb. In the process, he dropped his bottle, startling the monster with the loud smash, as the sound reminded him of other, more violent outbursts he had heard earlier in the day. The sound of the smashing bottle was rivaled however, by the much louder sound of the man screaming before landing on his ass which reeked of shit. The fallen man stared at the pool of spilled brown liquid as if it were a loved one stricken by sudden death.

Looking straight up at the monster in a defiant refusal to focus his vision, the man uttered soggy words.

"Yeah, I'm drunk. So what? Are *you* here to arrest me? Ha! Are *you* here to judge me, convict me, *sentence* me? Ha! Who cares if I'm drunk? I know what's going on. It's the end, and it couldn't have come fast enough, and if you ask me, being drunk is the only way to go."

Without any warning, the man lay down flat on his back, exposing his ample belly, for the shirt he wore was too small and rode up shamelessly. The man's eyes fixated on the stars above. They gazed back blankly, not even offering a face, or an opinion of their own; instead, they offered only the cerulean, dejected reflection of a sun now long gone, abandoning all below.

"It's not often that you can see stars in this city. Most of the time, you can only see the clouds that piss down on each and every one of us, unless, of course, you've been blessed with one of those crowns over your head."

The man accentuated those last words by aiming his extended arm, and firing the long, black, bleak nail at the tip of his trigger finger at several of the opulent roofs capping the unseen homes hiding securely behind the thick walls tasked with protecting them. The sudden extension of the man's right arm distressed the monster, forcing him to take a defensive stance. Ready to pounce, the monster quickly calmed after once again hearing the docile nature of the man's dejected voice.

"I never liked the stars, you know. Not even as a kid," the man said. "I actually hated them. Probably because I never got the chance to look up at them the few times they decided to come out."

The monster approached the man: a meal laid out for him like an overdone steak sitting patiently on a silver platter. He dragged his ankle behind him as he got closer, while the man, whose sight was aimed skyward, continued to speak.

"I was too busy working, or too tired after working, to look up at them. Now that I see them, I have to admit that they really are beautiful."

The man coughed, cleared his throat then continued.

"I heard the screams. I saw the bodies. I walked for hours to get away from them. It's funny how nobody noticed me. I guess I blended in with the chaos. And now I'm here. A place I was always told to stay away from. But now those who told me to stay away are all gone. Probably eaten by someone that looks just like you."

The man smiled, exposing a set of wilted, blackened teeth, and added, "And *me*."

The man stood, and while still staggering and shaking, he presented an imposing physique. Despite the protruding gut, the man's body was a stark contrast to the squalor of his appearance. He projected power, and while the light of his power was dim, it existed, perhaps in his earlier life, a life long-gone, a life long-forgotten.

Now standing, the man could have made an effort to escape, or could have put up a spirited fight, but the man made no attempt to escape or to fight; instead, he took a step toward the monster, vacating the lamppost's halo of light.

The monster approached the man with a step of his own.

"Are we that different?" The man asked as he ran his hand against the rugged terrain of his face. "I see the gash in your head, the scars on your hands, your arms, your body. Are they any different than the ones I've suffered at the hands of a world that, in truth, neither of us stands a chance against?"

The man took another step. His movements, while staggered, were determined, elegant even. The monster followed by taking another step toward the man, the sound of his dragging ankle interrupting the silence that took hold whenever the man stopped speaking.

"I understand why you do what you do. Though I don't believe you understand it. What you're doing is the simplest thing in the world. It's not evil. It's just natural. But it won't last. It can't. *They* won't let it."

The man took another step; the monster followed with another one of his own. One more step and the man would be in arm's reach. The monster knew it, and his hunger knew it, for it once again drove his arms upward and stretched them out toward his prey in rapacious anticipation. The man must have known it as well, but he still made no effort to pause, to turn, to escape.

"I heard, once, that the meek would inherit the world, but looking at you, I now know that isn't the case."

The man looked beyond the monster's sloping shoulders at the mountain, and the shimmering beacon perched at its summit. He raised his arm and pointed at the mountain top. Despite being near enough to grab the man's outstretched arm, the monster lowered his arms, turned around and stared at the glistening light perched atop the peak of the mountain. Like a bastard sibling, the light appeared determined to blend in with the sapphire stars above, but after a few moments the monster saw it flicker, while the ancient light of the constellations was constant and unwavering.

"You can only die once," the man said.

The monster turned back around and took another step forward, putting the man within reach. His hunger stretched his arms back out for him. His hunger forced his hands to grab and squeeze the man's throat until the vertebrae began to crack for him. His hunger forced his face forward until his teeth dug deep into the man's flesh underneath his collarbone for him. His hunger forced his teeth to tear off a large chunk of meat for him. His hunger forced his jaws to chew and swallow the chunk for him.

The man, pale with shock, staggered back, gripping the wound with both of his hands, coughing up blood that fell to the ground with soft splashes. Moments later, the man collapsed to the curb. Slumped and swooning, the man smiled before removing his hands from his throat allowing his blood to spurt and spill freely.

Enthralled by the sight and scent, the monster knelt down, lowered his lips to the man's gaping abrasion, and drank from the fountain of the man's life. The taste was sweet. He then thrust both of his hands into the wound with such force that he managed to grip the man's larynx and spinal cord. Fuelled by his insatiable need to feed, the monster tore the man's head off, and began eating it, while the now headless body twitched beside him.

When he was done, and there was nothing left of the man's head but a hollowed out skull and strands of thin grey hair fluttering to the ground like feathers slipping off the wings of migrating birds, he turned his focus to the body, eating greedily. Each bite, while filling, was anything but satisfactory, as the man's flesh was as disagreeable as his appearance, and while edible, it tasted horrible. After his final bite, the monster heaved and vomited what he had consumed. Like fresh cement, the old man's purged remains filled in the thin, barely visible rifts in the street.

Turning his back on the mess that had just doused the atmosphere of the upscale environment, the monster set out toward the illuminated mountain peak. He took a tentative first step when he heard a shrill squeak from behind. Turning around, he saw a large brown rat staring back at him. It hissed at him, revealing a set of dulled, vermilion teeth. A moment passed before the rat dismissed him as a casual observer. The rodent then plunged its face into a small chunk of untouched meat inside of what was left of the dead man's torso. The monster turned back to his original bearing. With renewed threats of rats charging at him fusing with his recent memories of his past encounters with them, the monster hobbled toward the mountain. Faint, flickering lights littered its surface, painting an illuminated path which he could follow to the top.

As the sky's cobalt blue grew darker, blacker, the light shining from the mountain's summit gleamed alone, as if it were a king, reigning high above everything.

7.

Exiting the genteel neighborhood that preached autonomy against the troubles of the surrounding city in a spirited sermon, the surface beneath the monster's ravaged feet changed back to the horrendous conditions that plagued the roads he'd travelled earlier in the day. Where only hairline fissures and slight shifts in the pavement existed within the limits of the lavish area, foot-wide cracks and cow-licked slopes currently seized control. It took tremendous effort to maneuver his way along the decaying road that appeared tormented by days of concentrated bombing, its gradient steeper by the step, causing the pain in the monster's ruined ankle to increase until it was a constant burden.

Following the dark route toward the light atop the mountain, the monster ducked and weaved his head to avoid the dangling wires that stretched down across his path, every wire singing a haunting hymn. The voltaic veins convened around green power boxes so overwhelmed with electricity that burn holes mottled the cables. The wires came from all sides, traffic with no end, a populous of power out of control, a tangled web weaved recklessly.

As he shambled onwards, the monster saw the shell of a car left mangled, stripped, and gorged. Moments after passing the husk of metal, he saw how life consumes death in a pile of dead cockroaches, and a multitude of ants devouring their carcasses.

The incline of his path shot up, pointing vertically, forcing his neck to pull his head back as if a hand tugged at his hair. The light above, his guiding star, had disappeared. The meandering path he followed led him through a small neighborhood that obstructed his view.

The only lights the monster could see, the only signals he could follow, were spears of radiance leaking through the smudged windows of several shacks that enveloped him.

Lining both sides of the path, the shacks were so close to each other that they appeared to seep into one another, as if a collection of ten shacks was just one large, shabby, graffiti stricken structure. They shared tin roofs, so rusted that even amidst the tightening noose of the coming nightfall their singed caramel color could still be seen. With crude walls constructed from scrap metal, the shacks looked poised to topple at the slightest tremor, yet they remained in place, resilient, surrounding the monster like muted phantoms.

An odor of decay wafted through the dense thicket of dangling wires, twisted tin, splintered wood, and molded metal. The monster heard nothing but the electrical hum echoing above the corroded streets until a faint shuffling from inside one of the shacks aroused his attention.

He was compelled to investigate, for where there was sound, there was life, and its noise, no matter how hushed, was the music that preyed on the monster's deepest, darkest desire.

He wandered into the collection of improvised homes until he found himself standing before a tin door. The monster smacked the metal door with his opened palm, the reverberating clang echoing throughout the area like a steel drum. When he stopped, the monster could hear the same shuffling from inside the shabby structure.

With his stomach stimulated to the point of climax, the monster smacked the door harder; the echoes growing louder, as did the frequency of the shuffling inside.

He continued to throttle the door, when he heard more shuffling from another shack, and then another, and another; it was as if the monster had stirred up the inhabitants of a beehive.

He left the first door and approached another door of another frail shack. He smacked it with the same relentless fury and was met with the same shuffling from inside the home, but not a single human voice.

He clenched his palms into fists, and slammed them into every door he could find. His hands pulsated, then swelled, and then bled, as the tin surface of the doors wore away the skin on his knuckles. Shuffling reverberated from inside every shack he harassed, but still no voices. Further wild swings against the doors caused the monster to suddenly fall on the hard, jagged slabs of broken concrete placed unevenly before him. The fall resulted in more punishment to his devastated body, particularly his face, which sustained the largest blow, as his brutalized hands refused to shield it, no matter how much he urged them to.

As a gust of wind snaked through the honeycomb of shacks, the monster's ears rang with the sound of the shacks' thin, tin roofs rattling loudly, before nearly peeling off like the skin of a tangerine, for none of the roofs were nailed down to the feeble walls that propped them up; instead, most of them were only held in place with fastened zip ties.

The monster's mind and body entered a state of delirium that extinguished any semblance of equilibrium. He fell once again. Slumped on the ground in a heap of hopeless confusion, he saw, through one of the shacks' small, smudged windows, a group of small, dark brown faces.

There were four children looking down at the monster, all with their heads squeezed tightly together. Curiosity overlaid their fear, like visitors to the zoo peering into the cage of a vicious predator. Standing behind the children, peering over their shoulders, gazing directly at the monster was a much older woman. Her face was lined with wrinkles, her leathery skin dry and shriveled.

Still the promise of food fuelled the monster, forcing him to his feet. On the other side of the window, the children scurried away like a distressed nest of mice. The woman however, didn't move, but stood like a sculpted idol. The monster attempted to smash through the stained glass with his swollen fists, but was unsuccessful, as his strikes were incapable of breaking the window encrusted with years of filth. He stared at the unbreakable pane, and stopped his pounding when he saw his own reflection. With grime shrouding the window's surface like a funeral shawl, the monster's scarred eyes stared at a startling image that perverted and maligned his already mangled face.

Dismissing the nightmarish likeness coldly glaring back at him, the monster continued trying to force his way into the shack. He moved from the window, and approached the door, which had a large wooden cross nailed to its face. Avoiding the cross, he pounded on the door with his pillaged hands, each impact more agonizing than the last, and yet he persisted, but the door would not give way despite its depleted appearance, proving to be remarkably steadfast in its resistance to his aggression.

Meanwhile, the shuffling sounds of life continued to pass through every crack of every wall of every shack, tickling the monster's eardrums, mocking him, driving him mad.

No longer able to endure the taunts, the monster rushed toward another shack, but stumbled halfway, his foot falling into a deep, hidden pothole that nearly snapped his leg in half.

It could have been a life ending injury, as the inability to progress forward would have eliminated the monster's ability to feed, but his leg managed to miraculously sustain the sudden drop, his body luckily preventing itself from collapsing forward, momentarily defying gravity.

When he regained his balance, the monster returned to the shack with the four children, the old woman, and the wooden cross nailed to its door. When he reached their home, he finally heard the voice of one of the children.

"Why don't we leave, grandma?"

"And go where?" the old woman responded, her voice calm yet filled with fear. It was a reserved, secure fear, the kind of fear certain people carry with them all the time. It was a fear born of life itself, and the harshness it constantly brings. It was the type of fear that prevents anybody equipped with it to succumb to overwhelming, crippling terror, as they are forced to fight it every second of their lives.

The monster recommenced his bombardment against the door, savagely pounding it; cracking sounds exploded from his knuckles as the bones struck and raked the tin surface, but still it refused to budge. Exhausted, the monster's arms fell listlessly to his side. He leaned on the door breathing heavily, his appetite burning hotter and brighter, as his heart beat faster and harder, inexorably pumping blood throughout his body, feeding his limbs through distended veins. In a final, last-ditch effort, the monster closed his eyes, and charged at the tin barrier.

His skull smashed against the wooden cross nailed to the door, creating large clefts in the center of both the cross and his forehead, but he was still unable to breach the door. He staggered back, gazing at the face of the old woman through the encrusted window. Staring back at him, the old woman stepped back and raised a hand, revealing a palm filled with deep wrinkles that looked like scars. She closed her eyes, touched her forehead, beat her clad, sagging breast, touched her shoulder, swept her hand across her chest, and touched her other shoulder, perfectly following the dimensions of the cross nailed to the door, before stepping away from the window, out of sight.

With the thinness of the shacks' walls and doors betraying the thickness of their resolve, the monster wiped away the blood pouring from the wound in his forehead. He licked each finger when done, turned around, and recommenced his journey toward the mountain's illumined peak.

8.

The beacon shining from the mountain's summit came back into view, enticing the monster, summoning him after a brief absence. His eyes widened, as the luminous gaze stared at him, and only him.

The pavement beneath the monster's ravaged soles had all but disappeared, leaving behind only small chips of hardened asphalt jutting up from the ground like bone fragments. The shacks had disappeared as well. It was as if he left civilization behind in the distant past in favor of a murky future resting on a pastoral path of isolation.

He obsessively followed the exalted light above, step by step, higher and higher, closer and closer.

He stopped, turned, sniffed, and picked up a scent reeking of rancid familiarity. His stomach remained calm. He stayed where he was, waiting, hearing steps. They were faint, but they were closing in quietly. No voices accompanied them. But after a few moments of listening, and the golden glow tempting above, the monster turned back and recommenced his journey up the mountain.

Reaching the top, the source of the golden glow appeared to be held captive, trapped behind a large iron door in the center of a large wall that stretched beyond the ends of his vision. The wall was made from brick, with splashes of mortar leaking out from between each block. The monster took a step forward, and saw a light shining down in front of the iron door, and much of the wall that sprouted from its sides. It was not golden and warm like the one that lured him there, but blue and cold, transforming the mountain into a glacier, with the monster standing at the frigid apex.

Along the top of the great iron portal, and the wall surrounding it, were rows of glass teeth, gleaming menacingly, daring anyone to trespass, hoping to taste the flesh of those foolish enough to touch them. Through those teeth, the light of the moon was guided downward, infusing everything around the monster with an indigo sheen.

Shuffling around, the monster heard steps behind him, plodding toward his back, beating the earth. He backed toward the great door, until his back pressed against it. He was desperate to enter, desperate to reach the golden light, desperate to feed, when the sound of the steps coming toward him grew even louder. Lowering his eyes to the path behind him, the monster saw the source of the steps that trailed him. A horde of fiends pressed toward him, their eyes vacant, their mouths open, blood slipping from their chins, staining the tattered rags that covered their bodies.

They had followed the monster up the mountain, guided by the same eminent glow that tantalized him. He stared blankly as they filed up the archaic path he'd just walked, each one staring at the light behind the door.

Then, without warning, the iron door gave way behind the monster's back, causing him to slip and fall. He managed to roll out of the way, just as a horde of men rushed through the doorway. All of the men wore the same dark blue uniforms, had on the same black boots, and the same thick, black vests that amplified their physiques. As they passed the monster, they failed to notice his presence, for their attention, like the guns held tightly in their hands, was pointed at the fiends lurching toward them.

The men's guns ejected casings, while their bullets cut their opposition down without mercy, but the monstrous legion kept coming at them.

The sound of the gunfire was rapturous, and with stored memories of the familiar noise, and their savage effects tormenting him as if he were struck by the bullets themselves, the monster clenched his body into a ball.

The bullets tore through the bodies of the hobbling mass that continued to press forward. The fiends groaned with every impact between lead and skin, but their resolve endured, as their numbers swelled. The men who fired upon them howled like starving coyotes; hissing and screaming curses, thumping their chests, declaring their superiority. Yet, despite their invincible firepower, and their unflappable will to use it, the sheer number of those they wished to exterminate continued to grow, forming an unstoppable, cresting wave.

At the height of the men's fervor, the thunderous sounds of bullets exploding from their guns began to make way for timid clicks that whispered weakness behind the triggers desperately pulled by the men's fingers.

The men's faces shifted from pools of overflowing confidence to ascetic crevices. Despite the silence of their guns' muzzles, and the chilling of their tips, the men continued to point and shoot absolutely nothing. Panicked screams replaced vulgar boasts. Some of the men twirled their weapons around, turning them into clubs, while closing the gap between themselves and the fiends determined to devour them.

Some of the men swung their guns wildly, valiantly defending those fighting beside them, laughing in the face of certain death. Others, cowards, fled, whipped by fear, abandoning their brethren. The fiends unanimously pulsed ahead, and as one fell, another stepped forward, inserting their feet into the fresh, empty footprints left behind.

"There are too many," one man cried.

"Run," another replied.

"Get back inside," another shouted.

The men retreated as they measured the madness through eyes stained with the blood of the slain. Their backs pressed together, they swung their weapons, striking whatever they could. Loud cracks and snaps punctuated the night as their blows splintered the bones of the fiends like dead branches. As the screams of their comrades continued to blare out, the men stampeded back through the large, opened doorway like herded cattle. Desperate, they formed a bottleneck, resulting in a single man, unlucky enough to fall amidst the horde of his own kind, who was trampled so severely blood sprayed from his ears, nose, eyes, and mouth simultaneously just before his skull was completely crushed by the crippling fear of lost power.

Panic coursed through the enormous doorway faster than the men fostering it. More men funneled through the entrance, stomping on the trodden man who looked less and less human with every fearful pounding.

The monster rolled over. Looking up, he saw leaning over the top of the wall, perched safely above the mayhem, the heads, necks, and outstretched arms of motionless men holding guns placed between the jagged glass teeth lining the rim of the wall. They pointed their guns down at the pack of fiends whose numbers had reached such a staggering amount it was impossible to see even a sliver of space between them.

The faces of the men perched atop the wall were different from those who had streamed through the doorway below. The confidence from which they held their weapons, as if they were extensions of their own bodies, was a clear reflection of the safety granted by their lofty positions. From up high, their muzzles exploded. Bullets rained down on the fiends like bolts cast by hated, yet worshipped gods.

As the men fired from above, striking fiends in every conceivable part of their bodies, from heads, to chests, to arms, to legs, not one fell. The fiends' suffocation of space forced them to stand side by side, dead and alive alike, huddling close, while bullets poured down on them like boiling oil. The onslaught was unyielding, as the men above pushed more bullets into their guns, blasting them out a second later, in and out, in and out, over and over, a never-ending cycle of brutality.

The last man rushed through the doorway, refusing to look back, ignoring the corpse trampled beneath his boots. The eruptions from the guns perched above slowed.

Instead of the steady wave of bullets that elicited a hypnotic purr wrought with havoc, the monster heard sporadic bursts of fury that came and went, striking random fiends with precision. As the noise of destruction diminished, the sound of the groans from the fiends took over.

The fiends still alive moved away from the corpses of their own, distancing themselves, while huddling with those still moving forward. Meanwhile, the dead were finally given permission to fall with pitiful thumps that clapped the arid earth like applause before the curtain's close.

The stench of the dead fiends stung the monster's nostrils, upsetting his stomach, frustrating it, marooning it like a stranded survivor on a desert island desperately seeking a gulp of fresh water, only to find themselves staring at a sea of salt.

With zealous chants of victory echoing throughout, the men above pelted the bodies of the slain with bullets, as puffs of grey smoke cloaked in a polar blue gleam rose from their muzzles.

As the large iron door closed, the monster stood, pushing his body forward, pulling his shattered ankle behind. With the fear of the fleeing men proving powerful in its ability to abstain them from glancing back at the bedlam from which they were escaping, the monster managed to slip through the doorway just before the iron door slammed shut. He glanced up, seeing the men atop the wall descending flimsy ladders, cradling their weapons. With the sight of the guns boring into his mind, and the images of their brutal effectiveness coursing through his memory, the monster fell to the ground and waited for the men wearing the dark blue uniforms to depart. Carrying their guns and ladders, without looking back, the men left quickly -- fleeing the scene of their crimes.

Sensing no remaining danger, the monster stood and walked into the compound, his eyes pointing downward, staring at the barren earth beneath his haggard feet. But as he looked up, he saw what such desolate soil cultivated. Stretched out before him lay a field of wooden crucifixes. Dangling from every cross, like festive ornaments, were fiends. Swathed in garments of flayed fabric, the crucified appeared to be dead, their gaunt bodies so decomposed it looked as if their bones were trying to escape from the battered vessels, the tips of their ribs poking and prodding their desecrated skin.

The scent of death was intense, too much for the monster to bear. The smell forced him to take a series steps back toward the sealed door where he could hear the sound of fiends' fists pounding against the iron surface.

The crucifixes were all precisely placed, like rows of corn, but ahead, beyond the harvest of suffering, there was the light, the golden glow that had summoned the monster from the city below.

He took a deep breath, held it, and entered the field of crucifixes without looking up, moving as fast as his crippled ankle would permit. Despite the strange desperation to reach the light that guided him, the monster stopped after feeling a splash of liquid strike the top of his head. He tilted his head upward; several drops fell directly into his eyes. It momentarily blinded him. Salty, the liquid stung his eyes, forcing the monster to rub them until the painful sensation subsided.

When he opened them, the scarring of his corneas was gone. Somehow the harsh content of the liquid had sterilized his eyes, purifying them of the wounds they endured.

He stared at the sky with a clarity he'd never experienced, and looking back down at him was a grimacing, male fiend; its arms outstretched, its wrists nailed to the crucifix, its feet tied tightly together with barbed wire, clasping its body to the cross, each thorn from the rusted rope piercing its skin. Groaning with agony, it was a breathing corpse, a defiled, battered body refusing to die. It was crying.

The fallen tears rolled down the monster's cheeks, seeping into his mouth. They tasted bitter, and he spat them out, sealing his lips like the iron door at the mouth of the compound, and walked away from the whimpering fiend.

In the middle of a web of wood and tissue, iron and bone, the monster smelled a foul odor that refused to be ignored; an insufferable smell that drove him to short, rasping breaths. Other sour notes mingled with the smell of the rotted deceased, clinging to it like a remora, bringing forth a familiar scent that recalled the dreaded city square. It was the rankness of shit that like a modern day Golgotha hung over the field like a haunted conscience.

The cries of torment from the emaciated fiends that were still alive became deafening, as they sensed his presence among them. The monster fell to his knees, dropped his head to the ground, as if performing a prayer, and forced his fingers deep into the drums of his ears, trying to silence the sobs of the condemned.

With his fingers still firmly speared in his ears, the monster looked around. Through eyes purified by the tears of the damned, all he could see was a dreadful, red rainfall falling steadily from the wrists of all the fiends hammered onto their prisons. The crimson rain fell exclusively within the confines of the field. Every fiend had a personal puddle of blood encircling their crucifix, a private audience, the sole mourner of the forsaken.

The monster stood, and took careful steps, doing all he could to avoid stepping in, or worse yet, falling into, any of the puddles littering the ground like landmines. One gulp of the poisonous blood would thrust his body into a fit of violent illness, just as it had in the city's square.

Carefully maneuvering his way through the field of anguish, where every crucifix flourished, nourished by pools of pain, the monster breathed as little as possible, doing all he could to resist the toxic stench of the dead.

Drops of liquid again pelted the top of his head, except, when he ran his hand over his brow, and put it before his distilled eyes, the liquid was white.

The monster looked up and saw a dead female fiend; her arms fearfully bent, fastened to the timber of the cross behind her. Her breasts were stabbed; each one stamped with a dull, brown stain from the rust of the blade used to cut her. As blood spilled from her wounds, milk fell from her nipples.

Curious, the monster ran his tongue along his dampened hand. He spit the milk out, its sour taste making him wretch. As he took short, staggered steps forward to escape the pallid downpour, he nearly tripped over a small stump. Regaining his balance, he looked down. Resting in the center of a pool filled with curdling milk and coagulated blood, was the body of an infant. The baby's skull was crushed, yet the rest of its body was left untouched. Killed to be killed, soaking in its maternal milk that it would never taste, the dead infant had the same repellent odor that dominated the air of the field. The monster walked away.

He neared the end of the field, and as he passed the final crucifix, he exhaled mightily, inhaling the sweet air found outside of the field's boundaries. Pulling his fingers from his ears, the sounds of fleeting life from the crosses seeped in, but he ignored the fading cries; instead, the monster fixated on an old building standing tall before him. It consumed his attention, demanding it absolutely.

The architecture of the building was modest, yet vibrant stained glass windows and protruding stone columns exaggerated its posture. The high reaching building climaxed with a golden crucifix perched atop its roof. It was the symbol he had sought, the golden glow powered from the illustrious structure's interior.

As the monster approached the building, voices could be heard from inside, stirring his hunger. At first, he approached the building's gold plated, twin front doors. But with no windows in the doors to see

through, he walked around toward the building's side. After turning the corner, he faced a looming stained glass window. Trapped in the window was the figure of a man draped in a smothering green cloak. Gripping a wooden staff in one hand, the figure cradled a large gold medallion that had a face of the man's doppelganger in the other hand. The figure had a golden halo wrapped around its head; the aura matching the medallion cradled in his hand and dangling from his neck.

The monster pressed up against the window to see inside. The figure trapped within the stained window diminished the light cast from countless candles that did not burn, but glowed with artificial warmth. Aligned like the crucifixes spread before the building -- and made from the same wood -- were pews where men sat, occupying every available seat. Those men without space to sit sat on the floor or stood, filling up the entire building's interior. Perched high above the men on an altar, behind a podium, with his perfectly coiffed crop of ink-black colored hair, was their leader, the hero. The man was dressed in the same dark blue uniform, with the same enlarging black vest, and the same burnished badge placed over his heart; its face reflecting the blazing lights inside the building, forcing them to shine their glow elsewhere.

Speaking at the men from the altar's elevated position, the hero gesticulated with his hands, pointing at the men below.

"*You*, why did *you* run away?"

A man seated in the fourth row of pews who the hero was pointing at made no reply; instead, he bowed his head down, and stared at the back of the pew resting before him.

The hero shook his fist.

"You're all cowards, running away like that. You even kept on running when the door had been closed behind you!"

The hero paused, before adding, "How can we lose a fight against these *mindless creatures*? They have no sense of anything, and we lost a fight to them, *how?!*"

None of the men replied.

The hero paced back and forth along the altar, returning and slamming both of his clenched fists on the podium, causing the men in the pews to tremble.

"*How!!??*"

One man stood from his seat and said, "We were outnumbered, sir. There were hundreds of them, and they just kept coming. It didn't matter how many of them we clubbed, how many of them we shot, how many of them we killed, they just kept coming. We *had* to run away. If we didn't, they would have killed us all. They don't care how many of their own they lose; all they care about is getting their food."

The man shook his head, adding, "The fact is, sir, we can't win. There are just too many of them."

The hero ran his hands along his slicked black hair, before placing one hand on the handle of a pistol tucked into a holster strapped to his waist, and replied, "We *can't* win?"

The man who had addressed the hero looked at the men to his left, then to his right, but all of the men stared down at the back of the pew in front of them. The man then looked back up at the hero, and said, "No, sir, we can't."

The hero pulled the pistol from his holster, and fired a single bullet that struck the man between the eyes, killing him instantly. The man's body collapsed, but did not completely fall, as the pew behind him caught him, causing him to teeter back and forth. The sound of the man's creaking spine could be heard from behind the stained glass window from which the monster stood. While he didn't catch the intoxicating scent of the blood spilling from the man's skull, the sight of it pushed the monster's rousing hunger to a point of hand-shaking, salivating tumult.

"Yes," the hero said, as he placed his pistol back into the holster, the smoke funneling out of the muzzle, "We will."

None of the men inside the building moved. Whether seated, or standing, they all remained motionless.

"If those mindless creatures get passed the wall," the hero said, "you know the flesh and blood of their own dead, and the stench it gives off is poison to them, and that field is filled with it. You know they would never make it through, so why do I see fear in your eyes?"

Another man stood and addressed the hero.

"We know they can't stand the flesh and blood of their own dead, sir, but neither can we. It's unbearable. And why crucifixes, sir?"

The hero inhaled deeply, his eyes closed. He placed his hands across his chest, holding his breath. Exhaling, he opened his eyes and replied, "I don't smell anything. And why crucifixes? Simple. It's the most effective way to bleed them out, and feed the field."

The standing man quickly sat down, bowed his head, and just like every other man sitting before the hero, he stared at the back of the wooden pew in front of him.

"Listen," the hero said, "there is no Plan B. There is no second chance here. They don't want to eat *some* of you; they want to eat *all* of you, and they will not stop until they do. We have no choice but to wipe them out."

With the sight of the teetering dead man proving too much, the monster's need to feed completely took over. He raised his hands, clenched them into fists, and pounded them against the face of the saintly figure immortalized in the glass of the stained window until they smashed through it, obliterating the figure's golden halo, and destroying the pious man's entire body.

Shards of stained glass fell to the monster's feet, stabbing the ground, impaling its barren body -- but the monster couldn't see it, as his eyes were blinded by lances of light that shot through the hole where the window had been. As if he had opened the door to an enormous oven, immense warmth joined the light, causing sweat to burst from his pores.

The monster staggered back, unable to open his eyes, frantically wiping away the sweat spilling from his overheated body. Unable to see anything, he moved around aimlessly, the onslaught of stimulation sending his body spinning into disarray. He fell to the ground. He rolled onto his back. A few moments passed before he was able to open his eyes. When he did, the first thing the monster saw was the hero standing above him, ire crooking the corners of his mouth. Surrounded by his men, each of them holding a large firearm in their hands, the hero reached into his holster and pulled out his pistol. But instead of blasting out a bullet that would have instantly ended the monster's life, the hero raised his gun, reared it back, and thrust it down. The hero struck the monster directly in the center of his forehead, reopening the wound suffered by the wooden cross nailed to the door of the shack he had tried but failed to breach.

The hero knelt down, pressed the muzzle of his gun directly against the wound on the monster's forehead, but didn't pull the trigger. The hero moved the gun down, rubbing its metallic mouth along the skin of the monster's face, pushing it against his cheek, indenting it, but still refused to pull the trigger.

The hero again moved the gun along the monster's face before abruptly pulling it back, and thrusting it into the monster's slightly opened mouth. Four of the monster's teeth dislodged and fell into his throat like little stones. He began to choke, his breath eluding him, his eyes beginning to tumefy. The hero didn't care, as he shoved the muzzle of the gun deeper into the monster's esophagus, blocking his airway completely. The taste of the weapon's metal shaft was similar to the blood the monster gulped throughout the day, but he had no time to relish the flavor, for it was suffocating him. He tried to vomit, but couldn't. With the monster's chest feeling like it was going to burst, the hero finally pulled the gun out of his throat. The monster let out a gasp followed by a coughing fit that culminated with four teeth shooting out from between his lips. The hero raised his gun and smashed it directly into the monster's face, rendering him unconscious.

9.

Lightheaded, sick to his stomach, the monster immediately felt an acute strain in both of his arms. He looked to his right and then to his left and saw that his arms were twisted around. His palms were pressed against the wooden surface of a crucifix's limbs, held firmly in place by large nails hammered through his wrists. His position was awkward, perverted, as if the torture of being on the crucifix wasn't enough. He felt an intense pain on the exposed skin of his legs just above his ankles, which dangled helplessly. Several strands of rusted, barbed wire were wrapped around his calves, tightly pressing them against the wooden trunk of the cross; their thorns stabbing his skin. He attempted to wiggle his body in an effort to escape his raised dungeon, but in moving he could feel loud pops from his shoulder sockets that felt like bursting bubbles from water coming to a boil.

Through crystal clear eyes, looking beyond his confinement and the shroud of darkness that had fallen over the air, the monster saw other fiends nailed to crosses similar to his own. They were all on a different plane than his however, for they were much higher, closer to the sky above, while he was closer to the ground. In the midst of the field of death, the stench of rotted meat swung under his nostrils like a censer, filling his nose with a scent he could not bear.

He looked ahead. Standing in front of him was the hero. The man unleashed a series of blows to the monster's chest, pummeling it, crushing the cage protecting his beating heart. The monster felt one of his ribs snap as the blows kept coming. His breathing became excruciating. He squirmed, but the spikes driven through his wrists prevented any possible escape.

The hero, who stood close, radiating lethality, raised his hand and punched the monster in the chest, furthering the pain of his broken rib.

"It's funny," the hero said. "I used to do this exact same thing long before your kind. Well, not *exactly* like this, we couldn't actually crucify people, but I did pound those who crossed me. I hurt some of them so badly that when I was done with them, they'd wiggle on the ground like flies whose wings I'd torn out. But with you I don't have to worry about nosy family members seeking justice. I don't have to explain why I did what I did to anybody. I don't have to worry about anything. I can actually enjoy it because you aren't even human."

The hero took a step back, and looked up at the sky, which had become pitch black, neither the moon, nor a single star shining down upon them; their blue glow extinguished, as clouds collided above, turning the sky into an immense, thick blanket of obscurity. The hero sniffed the air. The monster did the same, and caught an odd scent; the aroma cut through the callous stench of carrion that continued to castigate him. The smell was gentle, a fateful fragrance, a smell of things to come.

The monster looked up at the gloomy sky, the pain continuing to course through his body. The hero pulled his pistol from his holster, reared it back, and swung it upwards, striking the monster square in the jaw. There was a crashing sound followed by a shriek of pain. Blood fell from the monster's lips. Long, thick droplets descended to the ground, forming a familiar puddle beneath his feet. His eyes focused on the laughing hero, who spat out a clump of saliva that slapped his concaved cheek.

The monster's aching jaws yearned for the hero's flesh. His lust was not fuelled by craving however, as his appetite went dormant, but by something he'd never felt until that moment: rage.

The hero stepped back and admired the broken, mangled canvas he had created atop the large wooden easel before turning and walking away.

The monster looked down, and saw patches of dried up, starved grass, as the blood and tears that fell from the bodies of the condemned sullied the field's ground, scorching it, rendering it infertile. He focused on a nearby patch of dirt, when its smoothness was broken by a drop of rain, followed by another and another.

He felt more drops of rain fall onto his head. It fell harder, and moments later, some of the liquid dripped into his mouth. It was invigorating. He tilted his head back, opened his mouth wide, allowing more water to run down his throat. As the rain pelted his face, he blinked his eyes, making the field appear as if he were viewing it through an old, grainy video camera.

He heard a loud crash from the depths of the sky, in the midst of the thick regiment of clouds above. A moment later, a bright light barreled down, smashing into the ground like the blade of a flaming sword. The flash illuminated everything, including the crucifixes whose numbers had been diminished by the darkness, thus revealing their true number.

After more thunderous applause and an encore of another strike of lightning, more rain fell, swelling into a downpour. The rain washed away the remnants of the horrors of the day past, as the grime and gore on the monster's body, hair, and face, disappeared.

The small pool of blood beneath his feet at the base of the crucifix had not been washed away by the falling rain however, but seeped into the earth. The dirt surrounding the base of the cross softened, transforming into mud. Gusts of fierce wind blasted all around. The monster's cross began to move. Riding the breaths of wind, the rain's dampened touch spread throughout the field like wildfire, where the mud saturated by the blood that fell from the bodies of the fiends, gave the earth a rubicund tint. The wind's energy increased, causing the monster's crucifix to list to one side. He could hear the groans of those around him, as those still clinging to life responded to nature's fury. His crucifix shifted in its unstable foundation, rocking fiercely, as the mud continued to soften.

With the thunder growling, the lightning flashing, the wind growing more powerful, and the rain falling in sheets, the cross slipped free and slammed to the ground.

Lying on the cross in the red muck, the monster's face pointed toward the sky, the rain pounded him relentlessly. For the first few moments, the quenching water filled his mouth, but soon the vehemence with which the rain fell became overwhelming. He choked on the excess of water, forcing him to swing his head in a desperate effort to gain relief from the downpour, if only for a moment.

His body tensed, as the rain continued to pound into him, the pain flowing throughout his limbs. Without any other options, the monster tore away from the crucifix. Beginning with his legs, he managed to slither out of the barbed wire. With all his might he pulled his hands, and the nails fastening them to the wooden beam of the crucifix, until the metal spikes released their grip from the wood. Freed, he was able to twist his arms back around, his strained joints barking loudly, the relief revelatory.

He raised his ruined body up from the mud, but immediately regretted the deep breath he took as his broken rib bellowed in anger. Standing in the mud surrounding him, blood dripped from the wounds on the monster's legs and wrists -- where the nails remained pierced -- feeding the earth below.

He took his first steps, his movements sluggish, as he sloshed through the sanguine mud and pooling rain, thunderclaps and spears of lightning accompanying his struggle.

He was stranded in the field of death and darkness. Everything, including himself, slowed, as the mud's reach expanded, the rain feeding its insatiable appetite. He managed to spot the familiar beacon ahead, beyond the crosses of the damned; he made his way toward it, the closer he got, the brighter and more extravagant it became. Reaching the building with the glowing golden cross atop the roof, the monster paused, tilting his face upward. As if on cue, a bolt of lightning licked the golden crucifix, causing an explosion of sparks to fly in every direction like celebratory confetti.

He scaled the steps of the short staircase leading to the glowing building's profligate front doors. He heard the hero's voice inside, raised and maniacal. The sound filled the monster's body with energy. This time, however, it wasn't his hunger that rose up from the pit of his gut, but the unbridled rage he felt toward the hero.

10.

The monster pulled his arms back and swung them violently against the building's front doors. The pointed end of the rusting nails pierced through his wrists struck each door, carving a long scar across their gold plated faces, bursting them inward.

Remembering the intensity of the light from within the structure, the monster turned around, and watched as the building's blazing glory illuminated the waves of falling rain.

The monster turned back around and peered inside the building's interior. His eyes squinting, he scanned the enormous room, moving from pew to pew, scrutinizing every face he could see. Some were shocked, some were appalled, all were angry. When the monster finally found the face of the odious hero, contorted in savage umbrage, he stared at him with ire of equal intensity.

The hero raised his arm, extended his finger, pointed at the monster, and shouted, "Take him."

A band of men from the last row of pews reacted instantly, and without thought or delay grabbed the guns resting on their laps.

The monster stumbled down the steps of the staircase until he was back outside, where he could no longer see the hero's face. The golden glow from inside the building gleamed, lighting the muddy ground. Rain poured down on the monster; droplets slipped off the tips of the nails pierced through his wrists.

He opened his mouth, and exhaled, whistling through the gap left by the vacancy of four of his front teeth. The monster raised his arms as the group of men charged at him holding their guns up, itching to pull the triggers and lay him down. With his rage in a state of unbridled ferocity, the monster charged at the incoming men, hobbling and swaying through the thick, muddy ground that continued to suckle on the downpour.

As if in slow motion, the men continued their charge at the monster, their bulky black vests bouncing with each stride. Aided by the light shining through the building's opened doors, the monster could see the hate in their eyes. Their guns were all aimed directly at him, the tips of their fingers pressed against the triggers. But the bullets were never released; instead, they remained stuck in their shell casings, while the hero's voice shouted out, "I want him *alive!*"

Following their hero's orders, the men raised their guns high above their heads. The monster endured the first swings, swinging back, clipping the men's faces and throats with the iron nails pierced through his wrists, savagely scraping the men's flesh. In some of the men, he tore holes so wide death came so quickly no suffering was able to escape. Though the amount of blood spilling from the gaping wounds of the dying men was immense, the monster didn't waste a single second lusting after the thick pools of sweet liquid that formed on the ground, growing larger, fed by the tears of the sky.

The rain poured down harder than before, riding the gusts of wind, soaking every participant of the fight to the bone. Many of the men slipped and fell as they lunged toward the monster. An opening gave him a chance to jump on one unlucky man, and sinking his rear molars into the man's throat; the monster tore off a chunk of flesh, and spit it out. Searching for a new victim, the man he attacked remained on the ground, his corpse, giving way to hardened stiffness, slowly sinking into the cradling mud.

The men, weakened by the restrictions imposed on them by the hero, fought hesitantly, many of them backing away, confused as to how to fight without capitalizing on their malevolent advantage. One of the men, a grim smirk haunting his lips, dropped his gun to the ground, where it struck the softened soil with a faint sucking sound, and pulled out a large Bowie knife.

Moments before the monster sank whatever teeth he had left into yet another victim he held in his hands, he felt a sharp pain cut through his body, as the blade of the Bowie knife slithered its way inside and settled underneath his broken rib.

The monster released his grip from the man he held, whose life was spared, turned, and stared at the man who had just stabbed him. Looking down, the monster saw the handle of the knife protruding from his body like an extra limb. His rage exploded into a burning blaze. The monster spun around, swung each of his arms from opposing sides, and struck both of the man's temples simultaneously. The nails pierced through his wrists sank deep into the man's skull. When the man's eyes rolled to the back of his head, and his body went limp, the monster retracted his wrists, pulling the nails out with them. The man's body hit the mud with a splash, the rainfall doing away with the blood spilling from the holes in his head.

The monster turned and searched for another victim, when a loud, familiar sounding bang, followed by a surge of pain hit his shoulder. The impact of the bullet spun him to the clotted soil. His strength sapped, he looked up, and saw the hero's caustic face. He felt the impact of the hero's feet hitting the ground with every step, and heard him shout, "I told you that I wanted him *alive*!"

Standing steps away from the monster's battered body was a man with a pistol held firmly in his hand. Traces of smoke rose from the pistol's muzzle, while a hiss sounded from the barrel every time a drop of rain struck its smoldering, metallic hide. Sneering, the man turned to the hero, and replied, "I am not going to let more men die to save your fucking prize."

The hero stood face to face with the insubordinate man, wordlessly drew his pistol from his holster and shot him. The bullet smashed into the man's skull, driving him flat on his back. The other men looked on silently, and for a moment, as the mayhem of the battle ceased, only the sound of the crashing thunder could be heard.

The hero turned toward the monster, until he loomed over his ravaged body -- where his figure interrupted the rainfall -- knelt down, grabbed the exposed handle of the Bowie knife, and pulled it out. The removal of the blade unleashed a breath of fresh pain, a grievous exhale from the wound.

The slim slit between the hero's lips widened like the opening eye of an eclipse, and when it was wide enough for words to escape, he grunted, "Put him on his knees."

Four men dropped their guns to their sides, and grabbed the monster. Two held his arms, while the other two held his shoulders. The men propped him up and put him on his knees, which sank into the wet ground as they pushed him down, stymieing any resistance. Refusing to give up, the monster's mouth chomped wildly through empty air.

The hero stood in front of the monster's subdued body. The light from the building shined directly on the hero's face like a spotlight, revealing a smirk. The hero raised his pistol, and aimed it at the monster's head.

Staring at the ominous black hole of the muzzle pointed directly between his eyes, the monster went cross eyed. The pressure of the men's hands clasped around his shoulders and arms paralyzed him. Drops of water continued to fall, feeding the moist and hungry mud as his knees sank deeper into it.

As his attention strayed from the instrument of his demise, the monster stared beyond into the field of crucifixes, where the light projected from the building's opened doors shined on a horde of fiends stampeding forward.

The fiends gained on the hero and his men with remarkable speed. As the first wave of them streamed in, the monster saw a bevy of iron splinters poking out of their dulled, skeletal hands.

The hero, who was the last to realize what was happening, swung his body around, and fired his chambered bullet at a fiend steps away, dropping it instantly into the mud that readily swallowed it. The hero then fired again, and again, and again, putting down a different fiend with every shot, until the final bullet was ejected, and the only sound the hero's pistol made was the familiar click of an empty clip, followed by a splash, as he dropped the useless weapon into the gluttonous mud.

"How did they get past the door? How did they get past the field?" One of the hero's men shouted as he fired into the approaching horde.

"They smashed it in," another man said, dashing back toward the glowing building.

"The rain must have washed away the blood, and the wind must have blown away the stench," said a third man who was also firing his weapon until the final bullet burst out.

Soon, all of the men's guns began to click, chirping their weakness, and just as they had done before, the men twirled their weapons around, brandishing them like clubs.

With the four men who had been holding the monster's arms and shoulders gone to help their brethren, the monster stood, and stared at his enemy, the hero, who stood, staring back at him.

The hero raised the Bowie knife in his hand, while clenching his vacant hand into a fist. The man gritted his teeth, gnashing them together, and charged; each step sunk into the mud, leaving behind a deep footprint that disappeared as quickly as it was created. Standing straight, the monster glared at his storming adversary, his mouth salivating.

When the hero reached the monster, he took a swing with the Bowie knife. It grazed the monster's throat. The monster responded with a powerful swing of his own, the point of the nail pierced through his wrist missing his target, and tearing through nothing but the soggy air. The hero tackled the monster, the weight of the determined human forcing him onto his back. The monster chomped his mouth, only able to tear through drops of rain as opposed to the hero's flesh he so desperately tried to bite.

The hero, still managing to hold the Bowie knife, thrust it down at the monster's chest, but the monster was able to prevent the blow with a wild swipe of his hand. The knife slipped out of the hero's grasp and struck the mud, stabbing it; the mud responded by swallowing it whole.

Furious at the loss of his blade, the hero managed to push the soles of his boot up onto the monster's chest, crushing his damaged rib cage, while pushing his body deep into the mud, which graciously accepted the offering by sucking his body deeper into oblivion. The hero knelt down, and punched the monster in the face, speeding the pace of his sinking with ruthless abuse. Each blow was painful, the monster's face swelling, and the raging energy in his body dissipating under the weight of the hero's wrath. The monster felt himself sinking deeper into the mud's grip. After another punch, his head went under.

All he could see was darkness. The weight of the mud covering his face was immense. When the monster tried to breathe in, mud funneled into his mouth. His body tensed, then flinched, and then thrashed in an effort to end the suffocation. He went lightheaded, the sound of rainfall pattering above his consumed face, like finger nails tapping on his coffin's lid.

He tried to push his body upwards, but the hero's boot kept him down. There was no noise to make, no breath to take, and no escape. His movements stopped, and just as the monster was about to succumb to the mud, the pressure of the hero's boot rescinded, but his body couldn't take advantage of the release, and he remained stuck under the cover of mud, completely submerged.

Finally, using the last threads of energy he had left, the monster rose up. Muddy filth slipped off the contours of his swollen countenance. Even after his release from the clutches of the mud, he still could not breathe. He shook his head, forcing the mud to spill out of his mouth as he vomited pure earth. He took a deep breath -- glorious and painful -- before coughing violently, causing his crushed, cracked ribs to scream in agony.

The thickness of the mud had also completely sullied the clarity of the monster's newfound vision. He wiped his eyes, but regardless how hard he tried, traces of mud remained. The mud hardened around the edges of his soiled eyes, crudely filling in whatever open space it could, narrowing them, tunneling his vision as it attempted to only locate one thing: the hero of men.

Those left alive from the band of men tasked to capture the monster ran back toward the building. Tearing through the yawning night air, they galloped on the sodden, unfruitful ground, sprinting, fleeing, many of them looking back in horror, their faces strained, their eyes filled with fear, as they hoped to escape the fate offered them by the horde of fiends pursuing close behind.

The wet soil sank under the pressure of the fiends' steps, while they quickly closed in on the glowing building. The monster watched as the brilliant light shining through the building's wounded front doors was dimmed, but not extinguished, as the doors' closing was foiled by the hand of a single fiend. That lone hand allowed the rest of the horde to stream into the building. Moments later, through the now wide-open doorway, the monster heard piercing screams.

The monster's burrowed vision locked onto the slicked hair of the hero, who was also heading toward the shrieking structure. He watched as the hero rushed up the staircase before stopping just short of the building's open doors. The hero then took a staggered step back just as a wave of blood spewed from between the heavy front doors and soaked him as if being spit out by the building itself. Shaking, the hero stumbled back down the staircase, stopped, turned, and stood stiff, motionless.

As the monster continued to close in, the hero broke his frozen state and ran right by him, forcing him to spin around just in time to see the golden glow of the building's open doors elucidate the hero's escape into the field of death.

The monster turned and approached the field, keenly watching, as the hero stopped and looked around at the profusion of crucifixes that he ordered planted. The hero of men staggered, as a barrel of lightening cast exquisite light on the faces of those still nailed to the crosses. Yielding to the sight of the horror, the hero spun around, looking at the death surrounding him.

The monster was unable to progress further, for while the field's stench of death was gone, dispersed by the storm's winds, the poisonous blood of the condemned, despite its dilution by the rain, remained, creating an invisible, yet potent partition.

He continued to stare at the hero who was now screaming with madness. Those left alive on the crucifixes loomed over-head roaring in unison, energized by the presence of the man who had levied their sentences upon them. Their cries flung down on the hero's head with such heavy handed prejudice that the hero stumbled and slipped, and fell backwards into the polluted muck. The tears of the dark clouds fell heavily upon him, flooding his mouth, stifling his speech, until he unleashed a final, terrified cry for help. Despite the storm's fury, the hero's plea could be heard clearly, for the hopeless fiends ceased their shouting, savoring the sweet sound of the hero's last words before his submergence beneath the field's blighted surface.

11.

Curtains of rain fell so tightly knit they formed walls of water that closed in on the monster as if he were trapped in a box. He walked back toward the building; its glimmering light, heavenly white, seen shining through its opened doors. He scaled the steps. Standing before the gaping doorway, he was blinded by the golden glow. He took a step inside, nearly slipping on a pool of blood. The stumble caused the ache in his ankle to throb, forcing him to his knees.

Prostrated, he looked up and saw a large chandelier swaying tiredly from a thin wire hanging from one of the building's thick stone ribs in the center of the ceiling. Covered in crystals, the glistening chandelier avidly reflected the candles' false light.

Squinting his eyes, the monster disarmed the radiance of the light shining on him questioningly. An enormous heap of humanity covered the building's floor, consumed its pews, and spilled onto the altar. He was able see a small patch of carpet running from the entrance up to the vacant podium; its ruby red color masking the blood spilt on it from those populating the pile.

Noises abounded, from pained groans, to the cracking of bones, to the smacking of lips, to an unusual hiss. The building was awash with an orchestra of suffering that bounced off its walls, vibrating the stained glass windows that held their sanctified servants hostage.

There were electronic speakers everywhere, nested into the building's corners. A gleaming microphone rested atop the vacant podium, adjacent to a large book with leather covering. Resting between the thick book's pages was a thin, lacy strip of scarlet silk that leaked out like the tongue of a serpent. Behind the podium, several emerald green robes, with yellow crucifixes stitched on the back, hung on hooks. On one side there was a large organ with slim, golden silos pointed upward, and on the other side was a giant clock, also fitted with stripes of shimmering gold.

Man over man, fiend over fiend, the monster witnessed a demonstration of mangled unity that was as grotesque as it was breathtaking. For the first time, the smell, ferocious in its potency, did not entice his appetite that remained dormant, nor did it cause him to squirm and heave, for the mixture of the bodies' blood nullified both the poisonous effects of a fiend's death and the intoxicating effects of a human's.

Like a child trying to step into a pond of frigid water, the monster carefully extended the tip of his big toe toward the pool of blood. A pool that now spilled out of the building's front entrance onto the stairway in front. With only his toe in the pool, he was unable to firmly step his whole foot inside the building, for there was no room available that wasn't consumed by the dead.

A man, whose face was so ravaged, so scarred, that discovering his identity would have been impossible, suddenly emerged from the slaughtered hill. The top half of the man's body sprouted from the pack of corpses that mulishly denied his exodus. The monster stared at the man, who stared back at him, his eyes full of tears, as he began to whimper out pleas for help, caring little that the only witness to his petition was a member of the same band who had caused his suffering as retribution for the suffering he and his band had inflicted upon them. It was a cyclical sphere of anguish, an ocean of torment that was perfectly exemplified by the man's moistened, globular eyes.

As the man sobbed and pleaded, the faint air of his words brushed against every wound on the monster's exposed skin. The rage the monster felt coursing throughout his body had, much like his hunger, dissipated; now there was neither fury, nor pity.

Suddenly, the man's mewling was replaced by a hair-raising scream, as he was abruptly pulled back into the heap by skeletal hands that reached out from the mound and grabbed him, sucking him back into the mountain of mangled men.

Turning away from the mound, the monster looked up and saw a dangling statue, stripped, humiliated, and mutilated, wearing a crown of thorns that pierced his wooden scalp. The disparity of the statue was strikingly out of place amidst the building's sumptuous opulence, as if the figure was lost. There was a vivid familiarity about the figure; its arms splayed, and its wrists nailed to the limbs of a crucifix. The monster lowered his eyes, and stared at a large wound in the side of the statue's gaunt body. The figure's moribund facial expression appeared to permanently cling to the suffering of the inflicted wound, though the blood flow was dried up and halted at the hip. As his eyes scanned the bodies piled atop each other, the monster saw that many of the dead had the same wounds as the statue looming above them, but contrary to the congealed wound of the statue, the blood from their wounds continued to spill.

The monster looked away and saw a portrait, swathed in a golden frame, of a woman draped in a green robe filled with enough glistening stars to illuminate the farthest, most unfathomable reaches of the universe. Wearing an equally extravagant dress, the woman's hands were cupped together. Appearing to be neither condemning, nor condoning whatever she gazed upon, it was difficult to tell if the woman cared at all about the pile of slaughter in front of her, whose height almost rivaled her own eyes. The apparent acceptance painted on her face bore a striking contrast to the pain etched on the face of the famished man above. Unlike the serene woman, the man did not look down upon the dead with softened eyes; instead he looked up at the heavens with a bemused stare, as if he couldn't believe what was happening beneath his feet.

The monster looked away from the portrait, just as he did the tortured figure, and saw a large painting, surrounded by a sun-spun frame, hanging from the skin of the building. It was a battle scene where two groups were fighting to the death. On one side were those with clean, creamy skin, adorned with tunics, large, golden crosses etched on their chests, covering their hearts, and on the other side were those with dark, muddy skin, who wore no clothing, nor symbols. Portrayed as savages, emptiness was expressed through their pure, white, hallucinatory eyes, amplifying the apparent absence of any civilized thought. The painted battle was barbaric. Both sides wielded instruments designed for the sole purpose of brutally plundering the life from whoever stood across from them. No victor was revealed. With heavy losses on both sides, the fallen outnumbered the standing. Above the field of battle, littered with shattered shields and the gored, muscular corpses of the horses forced to participate in a fight that didn't concern them, there were long, wooden pikes topped with blood soaked crosses. And above those bloody crosses there were three angels. Buoyed by plush, feathered wings that allowed them to hover high above the melee, the plump angels were armed with nothing more than their golden haloes and their joyful smiles. Though the painting conveyed a nightmarish scene from centuries past, the art-work reminded the monster of the battle that took place earlier in the day, in the heart of the sprawling city.

Suddenly, the monster saw a group of fiends crawl over the top of the heap. Their crooked jaws clicked loudly as they gnawed on the chunks of meat dangling from the corners of their mouths; their hair made up of stained strands so soiled that the tainted tips glistened with grime. Their skin and ragged raiments blended in a menagerie of decay. Dried vomit spread across their chins and chests.

The fiends stopped, looked down at the monster curiously, and wearily approached him. There were four of them, their movements awk-ward, and their eyes empty. Hunched over, they moved like slugs scaling the mossy skin of a large boulder. Their bellies protruded as if they were pregnant. They were larger than him. Suddenly, one of them began to hiss at him, another flung its arm forward trying to ward him away from the vast amount of food they could never hope to completely consume.

The monster stepped back, until he was outside, on the staircase, the pouring rain pummeling his back.

Beneath his feet, at the bottom of the staircase, the monster saw three men crawling from underneath the structure's elevated position. They were all on their stomachs, and while their faces could not be seen, the blood pooling and expanding from their bodies spelled their end. The only choice they had was where they wished to die, and the men, who were granted just enough time to make their decision, ap-peared to want their lives to end outside of the walls of the carnivorous sanctuary.

The monster saw a straggling fourth man also crawling his way out from under the building. The man gasped faintly, each of his breaths stifled by the mud that grasped his body, refusing to let go, forcing the man to lift his face above the ground just enough to avoid its inhalation. The man crawled along the ground, digging his fingers into the wet, softened earth, pulling himself further away from the shadow of the building above. Claret stripes ran along the man's exposed back. The building, as if fatally wounded, began to bleed through the cracks between the planks of the staircase's floor, marking the devoured man as he slithered away.

At the bottom of the steps, lying before the monster, were all four men, their bodies barely moving. He knelt toward the fourth man, who inexplicably rolled over, exposing his wounds, moaning in agony. Sensing the presence of somebody else, the man must have thought it was one of his colleagues. But when he saw what face hovered over him, a face that aroused horrible visions of recent battle, the man withered in fear.

The monster's eyes swelled and his stomach churned, as his need to feed re-awakened. But just as he leaned forward, his hands outstretched, his fingers spasming with noxious anticipation, he frantically looked around. The ground was changing around him yet again, just as it had transformed from dried, barren earth, to the bloody mud, it now morphed into a river, a flood.

Originating from the field of crucifixes, the river surged toward the monster at an incredible speed. And while the yearnings of his famished belly went from a groggy groan to a curdling wail, he stepped away from the man he had intended to feed upon, and stepped back up onto the building's bleeding staircase. His steps, though painful, were swift, and just in time, as the river quickly overwhelmed the four men oblivious to the incoming tide of tempestuous water.

The water rushed the building, and in seconds it covered the building's floor, where it combined with the pool of blood beneath the bodies stacked on top of it.

The monster scaled the swell of rotting corpses, ignoring the airy hisses and the failing gestures of those who were no more than bloated images of the fiends they once were. They swung their arms at him, unable to move their bodies, as they were trapped in a position of gluttony.

When he reached the top of the heap, the monster saw that the water continued to rise, swallowing everything in its ascent. Water spilled in through the broken window he had destroyed earlier, as well as through the open doorway. As the water rose closer and closer to the top of the pile, the monster could hear the gurgling screams from those who were left alive within the mound; either fiend or human, it didn't matter, as they all were devoured equally by the flood.

Frantically looking down at the drowning interior of the building, the monster saw the muddy water quickly usurp the building's lofty altar. At the rear of the building, the resting organ began to play a twisted tune as the water forced the stale air out of its pipes before succumbing to silence after its submergence. A moment later, the microphone and electronic speakers were consumed. The emerald green robes fell off their hooks, floating atop the surface of the water like filmy sheets of algae.

With the water still rising, the monster looked around, spinning his body frantically. He stopped when something caught the corner of his eye. The large book once perched peacefully atop the podium, where the hero once spoke so confidently, was floating away. In that instant, the black ink used to scribe the words on its pages bled into the water and fanned out, creating a black slick in the midst of the rising flood, charring the surface like brimstone in the profundity of the inferno. Seconds passed, as the immense book bobbed like a fishing lure, before it sank, the slick of black ink disappearing after it, swallowed by the river's escalating power.

Just before the gold striped clock's submergence under the water, he managed to catch a glimpse of the frozen time, with both the short and long arms pointing directly upward at the number twelve. Moments later, the flameless candles spread throughout the building's flooded interior began to flicker before all going out simultaneously, extinguishing the golden glow that had bounced off the soon to be submerged crystals of the dangling chandelier. Then, all was dark.

Standing at the very top of the pile of the dead, and unable to see the rising waters anymore, the monster felt the river tickle between his toes. Seized by panic, he took a nervous step, slipped on the hair of a recently submerged corpse, and crashed through a large stained glass window.

12.

The monster felt the pattering of rain drops splashing against his back. He had not fallen into the river as he'd expected. Instead, he hovered above it, saved by one of the building's protruding stone columns that jutted out of the structure's side.

The air was cold, crisp, and breezy, every patch of skin not covered by his tattered clothing quickly chilled, forming taut goose bumps. As the rain continued to fall, each drop added to the frosty feeling causing his remaining teeth to chatter together. He wrapped his beleaguered arms and legs around the stone column, like a child hugging the leg of a parent, embracing it tightly, lovingly.

Down below, he saw the crimson river. Abominable, it was a modish *Acheron.* It grabbed and tore down every crucifix in the now liberated field, with the bodies of fiends still attached to them, screaming for their lives. The putrid river pushed them along like bushels of swamp grass. The current grew stronger, moving so mercilessly that *Charon* himself would have long abandoned his duties in favor of saving his own damned soul.

Marooned on the column, the monster finally managed to get a look at the entirety of the large wall. It was everywhere, on every side, a cage of concrete trapping those it was designed to protect. It was a barrier encasing all that was foul, encircling a surging flood of hell's high water.

Above the brick laden face of the enormous wall, the monster saw rats, thousands of them, all perched atop, effortlessly avoiding its acerbic, glass teeth. Appearing much fatter than before, their bellies hanging full between their haunches, the sound of their squealing echoing from all sides, each rat had fangs protruding from their open mouths, and red, ravenous eyes staring down into the corrupted water. Each rat sitting in wait to consume the past and spit out whatever memories remained, just as they had in the city's square, memories that would be quickly swallowed, erased, as if they, and the past that birthed them, had never existed.

Higher still, the monster saw a previously unseen bright light. It was so rich and dazzling it created an orange hued fleece that covered the entire compound, banishing the darkness of the night. The mysterious light was quickly disrupted however, when he saw a small radiant speck deviate from it, and fly toward him. It was not until the illuminated figure reached his face that the monster recognized what it was, and where he had seen it before. The fly had an orange, pumpkin shaped head. It hovered in front of his eyes, scrutinizing him. A moment later, it flew around his head before landing just below the nape of his neck.

The fly tore a small piece of his skin off, and immediately after, neglecting the soft tissue, it dove its glowing head deep into the monster's spinal column, where it began to gnaw on the bone. He swung his right hand around his unstably positioned body. Striking the fly, he killed it instantly, watching the insect's bloated body fall into the rising water, where it was instantly swallowed up.

Despite the pain from the bite, he tilted his head back up and stared up at the hovering cloud of orange light. He could hear the cries of the light. It was a buzzing noise that rendered the squealing from the rats atop the wall moot. More members of the swarm broke away from the group and swooped down onto him like falcons chasing their prey.

He managed to ward off the attacking flies with wild looping motions of his arms, the nails pierced through his wrists grazing the insects, while still clinging atop the stone column. But the hovering cloud showed no sign of retreating, and there was no telling how much longer he could prevent the flies from targeting him.

The number of flies attacking the monster rose; as did the number of flies he could no longer ward off with his swinging arms. Several of them cleaved onto his skin, and began to chew on his spine, where they relentlessly wished to break through the bone and consume the marrow within.

The pain was relentless, a knifing that sent his body into spasm, something he desperately tried to prevent, as the balance he maintained on the stone column was delicate. The amount of flies attacking him continued to increase, reaching a point where a smaller version of the massive orange cloud above formed entirely around him, creating an orange spotlight for his suffering.

With the rats looking on, waiting for their opportunity to join the feast, the monster felt a tremor. For a moment it seemed like it was a reaction from his body signaling that it had endured all the pain it could, a warning letting him know it was going to give out, and plunge into the depths of the putrid water below. However, the tremor did not come from his body, or even the stone column, but from the building itself.

The building shook more and more intensely, reaching such a fevered pitch that even the lusting flies retreated from his skin and bones -- temporarily alleviating the pain from their bites.

The structure was giving way. Beneath the orange haze of hungry flies, the large golden crucifix atop the building wobbled like a tree struck by a woodsman's axe before tumbling down. The monster followed the cross' descent with his tunneled eyes, and watched it enter the contaminated water adorned in its bright, golden sheen, only to emerge moments later stripped of its splendor. Cleansed by the flood's vile water, he could see the crucifix's true shade, revealed to be no different than the crosses impaled into the ground of the wretched field.

Like a crippled ship, the building began to sink, the slow speed of its descent offering the monster a small window of time to escape, though his mind remained blank and left him not knowing what to do.

As his descent atop the stone column began to pick up speed, the monster stared into the loathsome water anxiously awaiting his arrival; thick as tar, he could not see into it, nor was he offered a reflection by it, despite the buzzing cluster of bright orange lights glowing confidently above him. Fed by rain, fuelled by the blood and tears lathering the surface of the cursed field, he gazed upon a cauldron of sludge. As he got closer to the water, the monster could feel its warm, acidic breath.

Overcome by the stench, he vomited; the intensity of the poisonous scent too much for his body to endure. He watched as the bile discarded from his body was seized and pulled into the water's depths without a splash.

With his filthy brown mane dangling from his head, the water got close enough to taste the tips of the exposed strands of hair. Just as he felt the warmth of the water preparing to grab hold of him, the monster closed his eyes and slipped off the column, falling into the water's toxic embrace.

He felt a searing pain throb throughout his back, but his body did not sink. While several of his fingers were submerged in the rancid water, his body floated effortlessly.

Floating on his back, the monster found himself atop the once-golden crucifix that, like a calf refusing to abandon its mother, refused to leave the building that birthed it, even after its destruction.

He raised his hands above his face and watched as drops of bloody water fell from the tips of both his finger nails, and the iron nails pierced through his wrists. He drew his hands toward his mouth, his lips smacking in perverse anticipation, but stopped when the stench of the dreadful water reached his nose. He continued to stare at his blood covered hands and wrists, as the rain cleansed them.

Despite the immense weight of the cross, it floated like a raft, the density of the infected water keeping it aloft. The crucifix drifted toward the great iron door at the front of the compound.

The monster's eyes were hypnotized by the light radiating from the heads of the flies hovering above him, waiting to gorge on the marrow swimming within the bones of the dead. As he looked deeper into the cloud of flies, within the brilliance of their glow he saw a battle taking place, an aerial war, a dog fight between the flies and the droplets of rain tumbling down from the storming clouds above them all.

As his floating cross got him closer and closer to the large iron door at the front of the compound's brick wall, the monster felt a bump against the cross, followed by another, and another. He was trapped, stuck in a traffic jam of floating crucifixes. While the water's current allowed for some movement between the crosses, it was minimal, stagnant even, as they meanderingly floated into each other.

As drops of rain pelted his cheeks, the monster saw several fiends nailed to their crosses, imprisoned, their faces all pointed upward. Those still alive had their eyes wide open, their groans combining into a tortured song that crooned throughout the tempest air.

As the current pressed up against the crucifixes allowing them to spread out, the traffic of crosses cleared, allowing paths to form, from which they could move in directions that only the water dictated. The monster returned his attention upwards toward the hovering flies, and saw changes in their glistening cloud.

Like Icarus falling from the heat of the sun to his death, the flies fell to theirs from the radiance of their own swarm. He watched as one of the flies fell toward his chest, and struck his body. The fly did not fall like a tossed stone indifferent to the velocity of its plunge, but offered faint resistance, fluttering its wings in vain as it tumbled down. As more time passed, more flies began to drop, the resistance of each falling fly waning, and soon they all plunged down at a speed equal to the rain itself, resulting in a bizarre downpour of raindrops and insects.

A moment later, the monster heard a sound so piercing that despite the risk of falling into the lake's grip of avarice, he abandoned his balance, and thrust his hands against his ears. With his ears covered, and his balance maintained, he looked around at the sources of the sound wailing from all sides. He watched as the remaining flies spread out and commenced a vicious attack on the rats that moments ago were nothing more than boisterous spectators. Even with his ears covered, the aggrieved screams from the obese vermin, accompanied by the relentless buzzing from the swarm of flies, created one of the most disturbing noises ever conceived.

As the flies affixed themselves to each and every rat, extinguishing the brown color from the rats' dampened fur, and replacing it with a portentous orange glow, the two creatures together created a shimmering halo completely surrounding the encased flood. But it wasn't long before the rats fought back. They leapt on each other, using their dulled teeth to tear away flies from the rat beside them. Other rats, so tormented by the agony they endured, dove into the consuming depths of the water, or threw themselves onto the jagged tips of the glass fangs atop the wall. Absorbed and reflected off the pellucid glass teeth perforated along the top of the wall, the halo's light illuminated the fiercely waging battle. It was as beautiful as it was brutal.

Everywhere around him, the monster saw futile attempts at seizing freedom by the captives held within the water's soupy consistency. Bony fingers pierced through the water's lid, wiry tails wriggled from the surface like a stray lock of hair, transparent wings flapped helplessly, but nothing escaped the water's clutches.

As the war between the rats and the flies grew more intense, the light of the halo began to dim. The ample bodies of the rats began to break down under the relentless pressure of the frenzied flies. More and more of the rats' blood stained the limpid glass teeth of the wall, soiling them so much they were unable to reflect the light emitted from the orange heads of the buzzing swarm.

Still the flood's waters continued to rise, and the great iron door, which the monster's crucifix continued on course, slowly disappeared from view. Floating on his back, the monster kept his hands pressed tightly against his ears as the harrowing cries of war rang out around him.

Staring up at the sky and the storm clouds hovering above, he was abruptly struck, gripped, and flung, and without any time to react, thrown into the water that had a horrifying, yet soothing, comforting warmth to it that stymied the hardened goose bumps riddling his skin, and quieted the applause of his chattering teeth. While the coldness of the raindrops that pelted his face stung his tattered skin, the warmth of the flood's poisonous water absorbed the cold water from the sky and heated it up to the balmy temperature of its own. Still, the monster frantically thrashed his hands in an effort to keep his head above the surface of the water. In doing so he nearly sliced the skin of his face with the nails pierced through his wrists.

The curdling sounds of the war above his head bore down on him, and unable to cover his ears, the monster was forced to endure the shrieks, squeals, and screams of beating wings in all their tormented splendor.

He sank into the hemorrhaging water, while its surface continued to rise, soon to spill over the top of the wall, but it was not rising fast enough, and after one last gasp, the monster's head sank beneath the surface.

Just as they had earlier, when the hero had choked him, face-down in the mud, the monster's lungs begged for air, but there was none to be found; his death was imminent, and as his pain began to numb, he shut his eyes. Behind his sealed eyelids, flashes of recollected images appeared.

He saw the hero, covered in blood, sprayed onto him from the building's gaping doorway. He saw the faces of the fiends condemned to their crucifixes. He saw the baby and child he had consumed, and their father who had run away. He saw the coins tossed at him by another one of his victims, and the grey hair dangling from the head of another. He saw the slack bellied rats, their guts hanging low. He saw the cloud of pumpkin-headed flies gathered together like locusts consuming everything in their wake. While he saw those, and other images bombarding his brain, the monster's body began to accelerate dramatically. His eyes snapped open, were immediately stung by the deleterious nature of the water, and saw nothing but the thick darkness of its depths. He could feel his body being pulled, guided at the behest of the water's current toward the unknown.

By the second, his head felt lighter as his lungs shriveled shut. Like a ragdoll, the monster's body was thrown about by the will of the current, until a crash interrupted his momentum, as his back struck the brick wall. Drowning, he felt an odd sensation, as fresh air was lightly brushing against the skin on his back. Almost immediately the gentleness of the air caressing his exposed skin turned aggressive. The suction pulling his body toward the wall had grown stronger, and taking hold of his skin, the open air beyond the wall acted like a hook pierced through the lip of a fish, and tugged viciously at it.

Fighting against the desire of the water to escape to the open air beyond the wall, the monster managed to pull his back away from the hole that demanded immediate comeuppance. The force of the suction was unyielding however, and as his body was forced back onto the hole, he frantically thrashed his arms and legs around in hopes of stalling the inevitable.

During his frenetic gestures of refusal, a body hurdled toward the monster like a torpedo. Guided by the same powerful force that had smashed him against the wall, the body slammed against the wall just next to where he was stuck. He then watched from under the foggy depths, as the body's impact against the wall greatly enlarged the hole behind him. The impact appeared to allow him to momentarily cease his tiresome and excruciating fumbling, as the suction behind him seemed to stop. Then he saw the body, offering no resistance to the demands of both the air and the water, contort grotesquely. The body folded onto itself, snapping every bone within the now beaten sack of skin as it squirmed through the hole.

Suddenly, the suction returned, even more powerful than before, as the deformed carcass barreled through what was no longer a small hole in the brick wall, but a gaping aperture. Without being granted a chance to react, the monster followed the body through the breach, and rode a great horizontal geyser before landing on solid ground with a discordant thud.

13.

Lying on his back, his eyes clenched shut, the monster attempted to exhale, but his taxed lungs denied the notion. From the hole that spit him out, wretched water pummeled his face, forcing him to roll out from under the putrid spigot before he could breathe.

Lying away from the cascade, the monster opened his eyes. Feeling subtle gusts of air and drops of rain brushed against them, the stinging he felt beneath the depths of the water intensified, causing them to tear up. He knuckled his eyes with the tip of the nail pierced through one of his wrists, scraping their surface, digging into them like a spade's blade sliding into the earth's soft loam. Just as it happened before, his sight was once again altered, except this time the tunneled vision he'd acquired during his submergence into the asphyxiating muck gave way to an everlasting, bloody point of view.

He turned to his side, heaved and vomited the flood's poisonous water that he had swallowed, and even amidst the darkness, he was able to make out its murky maroon color before it seeped into the famished ground.

Though his body was stiff and sore, the monster summoned just enough strength to sit up, and then stand. There was nothing, and nobody around. Right back where he started, his attention shifted as another large hole formed in the wall, where a series of bricks slithered out of the moist mortar's grasp and struck the lifeless grass that lay trampled under the boot of the great partition. By this point, the sheer magnitude of the flood's body proved too much for the wall, and aided by the unrelenting rainfall the flood's level continued to rise. Moments later, water started trickling over the top of the wall.

The monster turned away from the wall, directing his attention toward a contorted carcass that lay on the ground just in front of him. Moving in short steps through the sharp pain throbbing in his shattered ankle, he got closer to the body. Its skin was pruned, its limbs clenched together in a ball. It was covered in a thick film that despite the rain staunchly remained.

He knelt down toward the mangled cadaver, his arms stretched out, his mouth opened, when the stench rising from the body reached his nostrils. He began to heave as the venomous smell induced a violent reaction from the bottom of his gut. He took several steps back, each more painful than the last, his weight constantly shifting from his ruined ankle.

Behind him, the water that had begun as nothing more than a trickle from the top of the wall had built up strength, and instead of drops falling like those from the storm clouds above, small rivulets of water began to pour down. Soon, the water cresting over the top of the wall flowed faster and harder, while the rain falling from the sky slowed.

The grey clouds above began to break apart, going their separate ways, as if they had accomplished whatever it was they aimed to do. When the rain stopped falling, the wind too stopped blowing, the lightning stopped flashing, and the thunder stopped clapping.

Feeling a familiar blanket warm his bare feet up to his ankles, the monster looked down to see that they were covered by the thick, burgundy water of the flood. Above, he saw the streaming water transform into a great waterfall that spilled over the top of the wall, splashing down onto the ground. Glistening under the revealed moonlight, the arch of the waterfall was spectacular, the freshly rinsed crystal teeth carving into it, forming beautiful humps that churned out water in perfect harmony.

The noise of the waterfall made way for tortured squeals. He watched as rats, who had managed to stay alive, despite the overwhelming odds pitted against them, could no longer endure the pressure of the disgorging water, as they fell from the top of the wall. The rats landed with a thud as opposed to a splash, as the water outside the compound was still too shallow to swallow their bulging bodies.

Above the expanding waterfall, a thick, misty cloud formed and rose higher and higher, throwing the swarm of flies into a state of disorientation. He could see that many of the flies, exhausted and weakened by their war with the rats, fled the cluster, stripping the swarm of its radiant power. As the flies disbanded, their relentless buzzing sound softening, the sight of their departure was magnificent. It looked like a spectacular explosion, with countless bright orange specks spreading out as far as the eye could see before disappearing into the evening sky.

Suddenly, the wall let out a creaking yawn. A large section of the wall, followed by another, and another, soon revealed what the sound had prophesized. Large fractures began to form as bricks were shot out from the wall like cannon balls. Moments later, those fractures became gaping lacerations, and the wall, beaten and battered by the will of the water, gave way. More bricks shot free, disappearing beneath the surface of the expelled water. So much water poured over the top of the wall, as well as through its punctures, that the flood, once incarcerated within the confines of the compound, broke out, liberating itself.

From behind the wall, the monster heard a thunderous smash, one so booming he nearly fell over in shock. The sound repeated itself again, and again, before he saw one of the uprooted crucifixes from the field of death pierce through the wall, causing even more water to gush out. He stepped backward, each step more difficult, more painful than the last, while the level of the water rose higher and higher around him, quickly reaching his knees.

He fled toward the same slope he scaled earlier in the evening, but as the foul stench of the water grew more fierce, the monster moved laterally instead, maneuvering himself along the side of the compound, where the water levels, while still rising, had not yet reached the frightening heights as they did at the front.

Moving along the side of the circular wall that wrapped around the submerged compound like a clasped fetter, the monster could hear the sound of the eager water's fury behind the crumbling barricade. The water would not be content with remaining at the top of the mountain's decimated summit after the inevitable collapse of the wall. It would flow down the slope of the mountain like molten magma spilling from the mouth of an angry volcano, until eventually reaching the impoverished tin homes that lined the torso of the mountain like a tightened belt. Despite the shacks' filthy, yet formidable defenses, the sea of slaughtered souls would have little problem demolishing each and every makeshift home, sweeping them away, as if they had never been there.

The monster reached the rear of the compound. While the water fell from the top of the rear section of the wall in the same fashion it did at the front, it do so with much less force, granting him precious time to escape from the pressing horrors of the mountain top.

The incline of the mountain's peak to its sloping side was drastic, much more than it had been at the front, making the start of his descent difficult. With pain coursing through his entire body throbbing more ferociously than ever, his first set of staggered steps down the mountain were a feat of accomplishment all on their own. Broken, he continued on, enduring the pain from his shattered ankle, and the sheer exhaustion from all that had happened. Dramatic bouts of dizziness came and went every few moments leaving him in a perpetual state of disorientation. Still, he kept going, progressing with short, painful steps, desperate to escape the chaos, to find rest.

Silence surrounded the monster as he made his way further away from the compound, and its ambitious waters. The air around him was still, yet moist, rife with the lush odor of a forest that had begun to envelop him, replacing the fetid stench of the flood above. The nerves in his feet were stimulated by the touch of the forest floor spread before him like a carpet of life.

Trees filled his vision. Large and looming -- even in the darkness of the night -- their intimidating girth could not be dismissed. However, with the power of the flood's water aching to make its way down the mountain it was only a matter of time before the roots of those trees would be infected by the vile liquid. The mighty trees would wilt before crashing down, and all that would be left of the forest would be a dried up wasteland that no longer celebrated the glory of life, but commemorated the finality of death.

Down the mountain he stumbled, further and further, when suddenly the quietude of the forest ended. The monster stopped and froze, as he heard a voice, loud and booming, blare out from beyond a thicket of trees and bushes.

"I hear your steps," the voice said.

The monster took a step back; the voice roaring through the darkness was soaked with familiarity.

"I know you can hear me," the voice said, "*You* couldn't kill me, and *that* flood of blood couldn't kill me either. That water took everything and everyone with it, everyone but *you* and *me*!"

The hero's words rumbled through the still forest air like a tornado of hatred. And while the words, biting and rough, meant very little to the monster, as he could not understand their meanings, the sounds behind the words, from the crunching of twigs beneath the hero's feet, to the drawn breaths between each pause of the hero's discourse, caused him to pick up his pace, onwards, down the mountain.

"I can hear you breathe," the hero said. "And I swear that when I find you, I will take this pistol that I found, use the one bullet left inside of it, and blast it through your skull. Something I should have done the moment I saw you."

Despite his efforts to evade the hero, the man's words got louder and closer, forcing the monster to dash through the blackened forest, his broken body and battered face slamming into the sturdy tree trunks. And while he tripped and tumbled through prickly beds of bushes the monster kept on running until his path became free and clear of trees and other obstacles. There he was granted ample space to run as fast as his shattered ankle and stricken joints would allow. But just as he reached a staggering speed, the monster lost his footing, falling face first into the moist earth.

With his breath snatched away from him, the sound of his pursuer's boots crushing through the woods behind him, panic set in. He thrashed his body around as the memory of being beneath the surface of the flood inundated his mind just as its toxic water had filled his lungs.

When he was able to turn himself onto his back, and air once again coursed through his mouth and nose, the monster inhaled and exhaled deeply before getting back up to his feet. But, before he was able to take a single step, he heard a sloshing sound not far from where he stood.

"Here we are, in another field of mud."

The monster turned from the hero's voice and continued on. He walked quickly, but carefully, doing all he could to maintain balance while negotiating his way through an open patch of mire.

With his bloodied eyes almost useless, only his ears and feet felt their way forward. And though he continued to hear the shouted words of the hero, who persistently spewed ominous threat after ominous threat, the monster was overcome with relief when his feet once again felt the tantalizing touch of the rich forest floor.

His relief was short lived however, as his exhaustion, that he so far was able to keep at bay, had finally come to a head. Even though he could still hear the hero's steps, breaths, and voice, the monster was forced to stop, as his body was no longer able to move. He fell to his knees where he began to heave uncontrollably, His chest near collapse; his lungs screaming.

The sudden burst of oxygen caused his dizzied mind to spin out of control, and in the utter darkness of the sightless night, the monster felt himself thrown into a pit of despair with no end in sight.

Standing up, the monster shook and teetered, falling several times before staggering toward a large tree standing tall in the middle of the tinted forest, its full figure made clear by the moon's soft illumination, giving the tree a glacial aura. When he reached the tree's massive trunk, his body gave way, twisting around, before falling backwards. As if floating, he fell, his back striking the surface of the trunk, slamming into it, stuffing his plunge. The feeling of his spine striking the tree brought back memories of his experience on the wooden crucifix. His back slid down the surface of the tree, where the saw-like bark chafed the ravaged patches of his exposed skin, ruthlessly scourging it. Soon, he was confounded in a seated position at the tree's base, his head continuing to spin, exhaustion rendering him to a state of paralysis.

"I know you're close. I know you're injured. I know you're weak, so come out and let's finish this," the hero said.

But the monster couldn't come out, even if he willed it, precisely because he *was* injured, and he *was* weak, even more so than the hero let on.

The hero continued to close in with soft steps, his voice a murderous whisper.

"I see that you've adopted silence as a way to escape. I know you're close, and I will find you."

Despite the hero's whisper, his voice was so clear that he was within arm's reach of catching the monster. But then the opposite happened, and the sound of the hero's steps, as well as his words, grew fainter and farther. The hero was no longer closing in on the monster, but walking further away from him.

"*Where are you!*" the hero yelled, frustration coursing through his shouted words. "Aren't you hungry? Aren't all of you hungry? Here I am, come on out, and take your meal."

The monster stayed silent, leaned up against the tree. Several mosquitoes, sensing his crippled state, began to wearily explore his decrepit body. They flew swiftly around his head, their buzzing resonating in both his ears, before they gently landed on one of the many patches of exposed skin, dove their elongated stingers in, and sucked out as much blood as their bodies could contain, while he stared into the darkness, into oblivion, through half-closed, bludgeoned eyes.

Using the tree for support, the monster propped himself up. With his body a checkerboard of weeping sores, it was impossible for him to identify where a sudden surge of pain and suffering originated. The pain, tenfold in its ferocity, showed no signs of relaxing; increasing by the second, it wreaked havoc on his senses. He began to vomit. Under the moonlight's gently glow, he saw murky blotches swimming in the fetid puddle before him; they had the same maroon color as the poisonous water he'd ingested during his submergence in the horrific flood. He staggered back after his body could expel no more, narrowly avoiding tripping on an unseen tree root. His body seethed.

Clueless as to how to placate the insatiable desire of his own torment, the monster convulsed and spasmed before tearing off every article of clothing he had managed to keep throughout the day. Soon he was naked, exposed, and under the pale moonlight the true extent of his wounds was finally revealed.

He saw the bites from the flies and rats. They'd grown to several times their original size, and they all had deep red rings like restricting coronas surrounding them. Wan puss seeped from each and every bite, forming petrified shells that plagued his body like pubescent blemishes. He saw the festering craters on the tops of his knees where rubbery patches of skin used to be. He saw that the skin surrounding his shattered ankle, where the bone inside had twisted and snapped, had grown as black and dead as the night itself. He saw rusted, wrinkled patches around the nails pierced through the skin of his wrists, patches that were so mangled, that it could no longer be called skin. Instead, the patches looked like the rotted soil surrounding a carnivorous plant whose roots stole the nutrients away from anything hoping to grow nearby, rendering it barren and cracked, like a clump of lifeless clay. The monster's body was a living, breathing, feeling, functioning nightmare.

The hero's voice was suddenly reinvigorated, springing out of nowhere, escaping the distance, and coming closer. The monster's anxiety set in, a sensation that sent his pain into a tailspin of suffering, nearly halting his breath, as if he himself were an open sore dipped in a vat of sodium hypochlorite.

Sensing the sudden nakedness of his body, the amount of mosquitoes that had fed on him earlier swelled. They swarmed him. While the thinness of their stingers and the preciseness from which they wielded them prevented the monster from feeling their bites, the moonlight illuminated their fervent feasting. Soon, every inch of his exposed body was covered with the small pests. They greedily drank the blood coursing through his veins, blood bursting with poisons his body had created and consumed, blood that killed the parasitic insects, causing them to fall and strike the ground like teardrops, leaving nothing behind but a plethora of itching bumps that only added to his torment.

"I will not stop until I find you," the hero shouted. "The sun will come up soon, and when it does, there will be no way you can hide from me."

With a reserve of energy that seemingly came out of a deep surge from within his body, the monster dashed through the darkness, cutting its endless black cloak like a searing blade, until he found himself standing in the midst of a particularly dense section of the forest. As he stood there, he respired heavily in an effort to catch the breath that eluded him.

As was expected by his brief, explosive run, the pain in his damaged ankle grew worse. But the monster kept moving, the haunting voice of the hero growing louder and then quieter with every passing second, as they both continued to move around each other in circles; the monster in hopes of evading the hero, and the hero in hopes of killing the monster.

Unable to see outside of the dimming rays of the moonlight, the monster failed to recognize the cliff hiding a step ahead. When he reached it, he fell and tumbled down the side of the mountain. His naked body curling into a ball as he hurdled through the darkness like a pebble swept off its perch. He bounced several times during his rapid descent, ricocheting off the hardened ground. But unlike the pebble that feels nothing during its tumble, he felt everything, his head, knees, hip, and shoulders smashing into the earth. The pain he was already succumbing to was augmented by his fall, as his wounds were instantly charged with each impact, as if they were electrical, and their power had been turned up to its maximum level.

When the fall mercifully concluded, the monster was laying on the ground in a heap of anguish, unable to move, as the pain of his body took over his senses. Much like his hunger had done earlier in the day, and much like his rage had done outside the home of the golden glow, now his pain had gripped him tightly, and squeezed him without pity.

Unable to control himself, the monster let out a piercing howl, which miraculously, though only briefly, alleviated the torment that left him quivering. It was as if the howl caused his suffering to evacuate from his body, riding his strained voice out into the air like a puff of smoke exorcised from a fire moments before its dousing.

Breathless, his howling faded, making way for silence, the pain again returning. Infuriated by his seditious attempt at dismissing it, the furor with which the pain returned to his body was incredible, for each wound, working in a torturous accord, seethed together in exquisite wrath. The intensity of the wave of torment was so extreme, so pure, that the monster clenched his remaining teeth so hard their roots began to push deeper into his gums, like mountains forced back into the ground under the pressure of a Titan's hand pressed down against their peaks. His mouth was soon awash with his own blood. It became so plentiful that as he avidly gulped it down, he began to choke on it, causing him to cough, and spit it out.

As his pain was finally reaching its pinnacle, the monster's shattered ankle gave out completely, and he fell, striking a large stone with his head. He felt weightless, floating, sailing along a stream of nothingness.

All he could see was darkness. Then blips of flickering light appeared. They came and went, flashing until they gathered together and formed a single glow that emanated comforting warmth where there was no more hunger, no more pain, and no more panic.

As the monster sank deeper into the pit of tranquility, diving further into his own subconscious, an image began to pulsate within the light that shrouded him. At first, the image was a blur, an anomaly in the stretching, bending light, but as the image tore through the light, the intricacies of it taking shape, he came to recognize what it was, as it took small, measured steps toward him. It was a dog. The same hound he had confronted and ultimately killed upon his own awakening. This manifestation of the starving canine was much larger however, and more malicious than the one he encountered. Staring at him, the hound exposed a set of elongated, dreadful fangs, while rabid froth formed in the corner of its hellish mouth. The hound's eyes were furiously red, like an ancient, eternal flame that blazed without interruption since the dawning of time. The dog continued to grow bigger the closer to the center of his mind it came, until it finally came close enough for him to single out the hairs on its hide, and feel the warmth of its huffing breath on his face; then it lunged at him. The corners of his mind flashed white, the luster from the dog's fangs glistening as he found himself gazing down the long, dark corridor of the hound's throat, and everything went black.

14.

The weightlessness was gone, replaced by a heaviness that rendered the monster woozy and weak. His head throbbed like it never had before, and all the pain he felt prior to his fall and subsequent plunge into unconsciousness, rushed back like a surge of adrenaline, causing his body to shake radically. Attempting to stand, he twisted his face into a labored grimace, determined to finish his descent down the mountain, but his efforts were in vain, as he collapsed immediately, his ankle still completely useless, the wounds covering his body wailing simultaneously, his stomach contracting angrily. He didn't even have the strength to keep his mouth shut, allowing his tongue, which had slipped through the crumbled wall of his lost front teeth, to fall out, and dangle freely, like an unearthed, sacred scroll unraveling over the edge of a cliff.

A gust of wind whirled through the area of the monster's confinement causing his naked body to shiver. With no source of warmth to be found anywhere in the chilly darkness of the night, he started to cough. Intermittent and shallow at first, his coughing soon grew constant and hoarse, before giving way to violent, unstoppable convulsions; they were like fits of laughter that gloriously possess people at the most unexpected of times, and just like those who became seduced by the spell of their suffocating mirth, he too was trapped by his convulsive coughing. The coughing showed no signs of slowing, his bloodied eyes bulged and blurred, the beating of his heart spiraling out of control, pounding like a hammer smashing at his chest from the inside. The coughing became more dire with every passing second, and he could hear the rumble of his own body succumbing to the spell.

As abruptly as the coughing started, the fit stopped, and silence was restored. He took a deep breath, doing all he could to take
in as much oxygen as possible to replace all the air that had been
lost. When he reached the point where he could breathe normally,
the monster looked around, and in an instant transformation, the
blackness of the night alleviated, and was replaced by a gentle, oce-
anic shade of dawn that contrasted mightily with the sonorous dye
of dusk.

With blue replacing black, the monster noticed a thick mist rising from the soil of the forest, like clouds germinating from within the
earth itself. The burgeoning mist grew thicker, as it rose higher. When
it reached his eye level, the moisture within the vaporous cloud softened his skin with its dampened touch, acting as a brief respite from
the intensity and constancy of the pain of his wounds.

Getting up, the monster wandered through the haze. Lost, direction serving no purpose, the sky continued to grow brighter above,
while remaining obscure below. With his slow gait, the monster staggered, and travelled a distance impossible to measure. Trapped in this
stagnancy, he suffered a familiar bout of anxiety when he, once again,
heard the voice of the hero drawing closer.

"You can try to run all you want, but the sun is coming up, and
when it does, you're mine," the hero said.

The monster tried to increase his pace in hopes of continuing his
evasion from the relentless hero, but the mist clouded any potential for
progress, forming an endless labyrinth around him, leaving him with
no options. Luckily, the incline of the slope grew less steep indicating
that his trek to the base of the mountain would soon be at an end.
Toward the bottom, the monster stumbled and nearly tripped over a
hardened object he had barely seen.

It was a tombstone, sunken and cracked, its color hoary, painted
with the gloom of erosion. The epitaph scribed in the center was almost
unreadable, as it was scrupulously faded. The monster took another,
careful step, weary of stumbling again, fearful that his next lurch would
lead to his falling to the ground, from whence he might not be able to
get back up, leaving him at the mercy of the hero, who continued to
close in, his words growing louder.

"I'm going kill you."

The mist began to lift, out of fear from the sun, whose rays finally began to shine through it, slashing it mercilessly, allowing the great, flaming star to once again look down at everything beneath it.

Around him, all the monster saw were tombstones, familiar crosses either etched in, or mounted on top of them. Many of the stones were so old, so crumbled, they were a faint breath away from toppling over, while others, fallen to the ground, trounced by natural attrition, showed signs of returning to the earth itself, as spongy, green moss covered them like fresh funeral attire.

The monster walked through the cemetery, passing through patches of crestfallen flowers that refused to bloom.

The air of the graveyard was acrid, as if the area was the mountain's personal lavatory. He smelled the methane gases from the long buried corpses emanating from beneath his feet, rising from the dead like the spirits of the departed. Neglected and abandoned, underneath the blanket of shrouding morning mist, it was as if those buried beneath the disintegrating tablets had been intentionally discarded, left to be forgotten, kept hidden like dirty secrets.

When he made it to the outer edge of the cemetery, the monster was faced with a rusted old gate. Both doors were swung wide open, where it appeared as if the opening had commenced decades earlier. As he passed through the opened gate, he stepped on a spherical object that nearly caused him to trip and fall. He looked down, where in spite of the burial grounds' best efforts to keep all it contained concealed, the monster managed to make out the forlorn countenance on the small orb. Practically bald, there were a few stray tresses of brown, curled hair sprouting out from it as if they were crooked blades of desiccated grass. Attached to the head was a tiny, naked body, and despite its appearance as a person, the figure was not human. It was a plastic doll. Filthy and dilapidated, the diminutive toy, despite its decay, had a pair of pristine glass eyes that had refused to succumb to the indignities of its body and the injuries to its head. The eyes stared up, far beyond the monster and the melancholy of the graveyard, far beyond the sun's apathetic rays, perhaps even through the heavens, deep into the cosmos, into forever.

The monster passed through the opened gateway, and as he left the orphanage of the dead, whose occupants would forever be swept under the rug of time, he sensed a sudden shift in the scent of the air. No longer was the air full of mildewed death; instead, it was ripe with the moisture of life.

The forest cloaked the monster, just as the mist did with the crumbling memorials of the cemetery. The foliage of the canopy covered his nude, wounded body, preventing the full strength of the sun's morning glory to reach and warm him, keeping him in the moisture, where only slivers of sunlight grazed his skin, tickling it, teasing it with its diminished glare.

He could hear the hero closing in, stumbling and falling over the cemetery's headstones.

Feeling heavy, the monster's body lusted for rest, but he ignored the allure of long awaited relief and kept going until the ground beneath his feet finally flattened, for he had reached the bottom of the mountain.

In front of the monster was a marsh. Tiny drops of morning dew dangled from the tips of every loose leaf; like priceless gems, they absorbed and transformed the light of the shining sun before releasing it in a beautiful cabaret of marvelous radiance.

He took a series of tepid steps through the flourishing land, looking at the odd collection of trees that appeared to tilt forward, as if bowing to something he could not yet see. After a few more steps, each one causing more pain to surge throughout his broken body, and each one making him more tired than the last, the monster finally saw what was inspiring the low bowing of the trees.

A lake, large and round, filled with translucent fresh water lay before him. With nary a ripple, the water was still and calm. Standing before the shores of the glassy basin, the monster listened to the sound of its timid tide gently sweep along the soft-sanded beach, before quietly receding.

He took a small step forward, just enough for his ravaged feet to touch the ductile sand; its malleability allowing both of his feet to sink under the weight of his suffering. When the tide returned, the water, cold but fresh, soaked his feet, and refreshed his spirit. The monster fell to his knees, sinking into the soft shoals of the beach where he felt the receded water return once again, and soak more of his dismal skin.

He plunged his face deep into the clear, azure water that gloriously caressed the sun's luminous stare, soaking every strand of his soiled brown hair. Then he heard a noise, and he quickly rose to his feet.

The monster turned, and standing before him, appearing as haggard, and as broken as he, was the hero. The man's brow was furrowed, his stained face filled with unbridled hatred, his eyes fuming, his nostrils flaring. His mouth was sealed, furious breaths whistling from between the man's crusted lips.

The black vest the hero once wore was gone, taking with it the golden badge covering his heart, deteriorating the man's true shape and size, while the jet black polish in his slicked back hair had been washed away, revealing wildly tousled, filthy, faded grey locks.

In the hero's right hand, he tenderly held a tarnished pistol, its oxidized muzzle pointed directly at the softened ground beneath the hero's boots that were covered in the mud he had tracked throughout the man's dogged pursuit of the monster.

The monster raised both of his hands, exposing the long nails pierced through his wrists, and the accumulated, caramelized rust caked all around them. He lunged at the hero, saliva streaming from his gaping mouth onto the sand below his feet. He threw both of his hands toward the hero's throat, while the nails, replacing the teeth he had lost, acted as a pair of iron fangs. The monster landed his first blow, catching the hero squarely in the neck, momentarily satisfying the iron fangs' appetite. But despite the depths the nails dug in, the hero charged back at the monster, and managed to grab his throat with his free hand, squeezing it tightly. The monster yelped out several labored groans, wildly thrashing his naked body, swinging his iron fangs with reckless abandon. But despite the monster's best, worst intentioned efforts, his iron fangs were never granted another opportunity to taste the hero's flesh, as the hero raised his hand that clutched his pistol, while still firmly gripping the monster's throat with the other, and thunderously slammed the butt down against the top of the monster's skull, crashing him to the ground.

The monster rose to his knees and managed to stand erect, his battered, bloodied eyes gazing at the hero, whose free hand was now tightly wrapped around his own throat, blood leaking out through the gaps between his filthy fingers. After taking a deep breath, the hero, who was trembling, and teetering back and forth, removed his hand from his throat, exposing a gash that gaped open like a wide smile, allowing the wound to bleed freely.

The hero raised his other hand, and fired the pistol that he held in his grasp.

The bullet's journey began at the skin of the monster's battered forehead, before effortlessly passing through the bone of his cranium. It swam through a swirling pool of cerebrospinal fluid, before barreling through the frontal lobe of his brain, where it smashed his thoughts, and destroyed the memories from throughout the day, severing whatever was left of his humanity, before piercing through the insular cortex, where it finally, mercifully eliminated all of his pain. The bullet then funneled through his temporal lobe, rendering him completely deaf, and extinguishing the enticing odor of the blood spilling from the hero's wound. The bullet then coursed through his parietal lobe, paralyzing him, before blasting out the back of his skull, where a stream of blood and fragments of bone and brain flew out from the exit wound and fell into the water behind him with soft, tiny splashes, breaching the peace of the secluded lake, sullying its clarity. As he fell backwards into the lake, the monster left behind a strident splash that created a flurry of ripples that proliferated throughout the isolated body of water, and as his body began to sink beneath the surface, the monster focused directly into the sun's golden glow, and from blinding light came pure darkness.

ACKNOWLEDGEMENTS

I would like to thank Montag Press for giving me my first shot. Thank you Charlie. Nicholas Morine, your help was invaluable, thank you. David Rogers, it was amazing to see my words manifested through your work, thank you. Lisa Hill, who has been a dear friend for more than half my life, and pushed me even when I strayed, thank you. Alain "B" Graham, who was the closest thing to a mentor I ever had, and while the time I spent learning from you was short, and it's been a long time since we spoke, the impact of your lessons remain. Mi familia y mis carnales, saben quienes son, gracias por todo. I would also like to thank all of the artists whose works and lives have inspired and taught me. There are simply too many of you to name, but know your impacts are felt individually. Finally, I would like to acknowledge the Mexican police force.

If you would like to contact Jonathan R. Rose directly, you can email him at jonan.rose@gmail.com

Manufactured by Amazon.ca
Acheson, AB

12314126R00069